Orchid's Bloom

Author
Roxann Gump O'Brien

Published by Rondell Glenn Publishing
Printed and bound in the United States

Orchid's Bloom
ISBN 0-9770026-0-8

This book is dedicated to the memory of my mother
Marjorie Grace Gump
And to the young ladies who follow in our footsteps;
Alicia, Jasmine, Lauren and Noelle

Chapter 1

2002

My sister's words rang in my head as I drove the twenty eight miles to Mother's apartment. Zandra had said, "Mom's feet are cold. Burnie has been here and had to leave. You better hurry." When I saw my mother, I went to her, kissed her and said, "Mom, it's time to go see Jesus and Grandma Gump."

I sat down beside Zandra and told her my daughter Rachel went to the doctor yesterday about her suspected pregnancy and I forgot to call. So I called Rachel at work. As I was talking to Rachel, Doris, the home care woman, came in and cleaned out mother's mouth. Mother started coughing. I could see the phlegm in her mouth. I hung up the phone.

Zandra said, "Of all the books we have read, why didn't anyone write about dying as being like this?"

She jumped up and left the room, stood in the doorway and then went for a towel Doris asked for. Doris stood in front of Mom so I could not see her face. Mother coughed again. She took one last deep breath and it was over.

Doris said, "She is gone." She went to the phone to call hospice.

Zandra said, "That's unbelievable; you were talking to Rachel about the next generation just as Mother was leaving us."

Doris hugged Zandra and me and we all held hands over mother's body as Doris led us in prayer. A hospice nurse arrived and she and Doris began to prepare Mother's body.

Zandra grabbed the tissue box and we went and sat on Mother's patio bench and cried. The sky was so blue it broke my heart. A wren was singing in the trees. My mother had just died.

I had imagined what it would have been like to endure the pain of watching my mother die. I now know. My mother, Marjorie, spent twenty years preparing me for this day. Twenty years of preparation was not close to being enough, for there is no way to prepare for death of the person who gave me life. The one person always on my side no matter what misfortune I found myself in. The woman who taught me to cook, to love flowers, to be polite, to be on time, to always make my bed, to give unconditional love, and to believe in God, died on that glorious summer morning. A chunk of me died with that last powerful breath.

I thought I was prepared for mother leaving me. She had signed her living will as early as 1985; her entire memorial service had been ready for several years. Hymns chosen with care-including their page numbers-Bible verses chosen with even more care-and updated within the last year. Cookies and tea were arranged with the ladies of the church. Money was set aside for a family dinner at "Nick's Rib Room" in Fort Wayne after the memorial service. Arrangements were made and paid for to have her body sent to the Indiana University Medical School in Indianapolis. Most of her belongings had been dispersed.

Content of drawers had been sorted and cleaned. Favorite pieces of jewelry and clothing were given to those she had intended to have them. Every detail had been thought out to make her death easy on us many years before the actual day. What we were not prepared for was the death process.

I thought about what Zandra said as mother was dying, how some-one should write this down because we had never read about the death process. Since I'm the oldest, I decided I would write about Mother's death. But I could not write about her death and not write about her life. And I could not write about her life and not write about my own.

Mother was a teacher for thirty years, not counting the years she spent teaching life to my brother and sister and me. Her private life spent with us was far more difficult than her professional life. I am the oldest of her three children by far, ten years older than my sister, Zandra, and thirteen years older than my brother, Burnell. Those ten years when I had Mother all to myself were very trying years. There was devastating illness, infidelity, unstable employment and wanderlust. I thought it was a great adventure and always filled with love.

Chapter 2

1938

$\mathcal{My}$ parents married in northern Indiana on a chilly, April, Sunday in 1938. Mother glowed with happiness. The tiny two by three-inch black and white photograph shows her laughing as her wedding veil billowed in the wind. My father, standing next to Mother, is very handsome in his black suit and tie. Married in a tiny white wooden church named Pleasant Hill, it was a formal wedding with four bridesmaids and a flower girl. A reception followed at the Gump family farm down the road.

More than fifty years later, Mother told me her own mother did not attend this wedding because my father came from a family who did not meet Grandma Fogel's "standards." I think one of the things that Grandma Fogel, disliked about my father's family was their strict religious life. Grandma Fogel was "United Methodist" and not particularly religious. Church was alright for social occasions but not for every Sunday. My father's family, the Gumps, were of the "Church of the Brethren." Considered very religious, they were plain and unassuming. The Gumps were well-educated. They also traveled within the United States, usually on church business. However, the Gump's did not wear jewelry, drink hard liquor, or play cards. They didn't believe in "fancy" things. Grandpa Gump was not just a farmer. He was a timekeeper for the railroad that ran through the nearby town of Garrett and he was a lay minister in his church.

The Fogels, on the other hand, were Indiana dirt farmers. Mother always considered her family poor. Grandma Fogel attended college. A college education was not a popular thing for a woman in Indiana farm country at the turn of the twentieth century. Her brothers gave her the money to attend. She was to be a teacher, which only took about six weeks of study in those days. Sidney Fogel talked her into getting married after the fourth week of study and she never completed the course, a decision

I'm sure they both regretted their whole lives. Grandma dominated Grandpa. At their fiftieth wedding anniversary party, he was asked if he would do it all again. Sid replied, "Tain't likely."

Even though her own mother did not attend my mother's wedding, her father, Sidney, did and gave her away. Mother's older sister Melba married a doctor, Grandma Fogel's dream for all her daughters. My mother borrowed money from Melba's husband, Andy, in order to buy a wedding dress. She paid Andy back as soon as school started that fall. Andy had also loaned Mother money for college. Because of him, she was able to become an Indiana licensed teacher. But she married a farmer with two years of college and therefore, she disappointed her mother. Much later in their lives, Grandma Fogel grew to care about and rely on my father a great deal. I would never have guessed at these underlying currents if mother had not told me about them. A theme I heard all my life was; "It's just as easy to love a rich man as to love a poor one." Perhaps, money was really the root of these underlying feelings.

Mother and Dad knew each other as children because they lived in the same rural area, went to the same school and sometimes saw each other at community functions. In college they became friends and started seeing each other as more than just neighbors.

They both graduated from Manchester College with a two-year Normal Degree in Elementary Education. Mother started her teaching career in a tiny country school near Fort Wayne. She lived in Fort Wayne where she rented a room with a family. With her first pay check, she bought a navy blue dress with a wide red diagonal stripe from shoulder to hip and thought she was the "cat's meow." Although Dad also taught, he continued working and living on the family farm near Churubusco. Dad came into the city to see Marjorie at every opportunity. By 1938, they were in love and married.

Chapter 3

I was born in September 1940. The story was recounted to me many times how my parents had taken a walk down a country lane late on a Sunday afternoon to enjoy the cooling weather of early fall. On the way back to the house, Mother's water broke. Dad drove her into Fort Wayne and I was born at St. Joseph Hospital. A week later Mom and I returned to the little rented house where they lived. There was not much money. Mom was not working because married women with children were not offered teaching jobs.

My father was never satisfied with his life. I don't think he was ever completely happy for very long. He bought a farm for three thousand dollars during my first couple of years of life. On this farm he raised some livestock and planted fields of corn and wheat.

A favorite family story is of me and a lamb named Annie Lamb drinking out of the same bottle. After just a year, Dad sold that farm for five times more than what it had cost him. My parents thought they were rich. They rented a cute little white house a couple of miles from the farm. My first memory is of being in this house when my mother fell down the wooden basement stairs with a pale green glass Coke bottle in her hand. I sat on the steps and watched her as she lay on a small cot in the basement catching her breath and rubbing her bruises. I was two years old and very frightened. Mother was twenty-seven and full of the zest for life.

When I was three, Grandpa Gump retired from the railroad and sold their farm. At that same time, we moved to a farm down the road. This house was big enough for two families, so Grandpa and Grandma Gump moved in with us while waiting for their house to be ready to move to New Paris. With live-in help from Grandma Gump, Mother went back to teaching school.

My memories of Grandpa at the time are fuzzy. He never seemed to be there. When he was home, he let me sit on his crossed leg and hold his hands as he bounced me up and down and gave me horsy rides.

Grandma Gump was soft and safe. A short round woman who held me on her lap and sang hymns or fed me apple scrapings. Her voice was gentle and she endlessly hummed to herself. I knew without being told she loved me beyond understanding.

Grandma always wore a bib type apron with pockets. In the pockets she kept a cloth hanky and little bits of things she picked up during the day, like her thimble and thread, a short pencil, or hair pins. She wore her uncut gray hair pulled back in a bun and pinned it securely with wide hair pins that sometimes fell out.

While I stood on a chair beside her, I loved to watch Grandma Gump make pie crust. She would put the ball of dough right in the middle of a little flour she had sprinkled around. With her rolling pin she would start rolling out the thin round crust. The most noise she ever made was banging that rolling pin around. When the crust looked perfect to me, she would pick it up, toss it over and roll it again. The top crust for a fruit pie was special. It was absolutely necessary to have a design cut into it. I didn't understand why. I just knew she made a beautiful design in just a couple of strokes with her knife. She would carefully place it over the pie filling and then hold the entire pie up in one hand while she took a knife and quickly cut off the extra crust. She would then take that extra crust and sprinkle it with cinnamon and sugar and baked them into pieces of warm sweet crusts only for me.

Several times a day in between doing her hand sewing, Grandma took a few minutes to sit down and read her Bible. She held me on her lap and told me stories about Jesus; she told me stories about my Daddy when he was little like me. She never told me "no." She was the kindest, gentlest woman I ever knew.

Grandma and Grandpa Gump slept upstairs. We all shared the large living room, dining room, kitchen and one bathroom. The bathroom in this farmhouse was off the kitchen. I have several memories of our farmhouse bathroom, especially of Mother washing my hair. I screamed the entire time because I just knew I would go down the drain when she pulled out the little rubber plug. The bathtub was large. I wore Sweetheart Soap on a rope around my neck and that soap could float. I loved those baths as long as I got out of the tub before the plug on the end of the chain was pulled.

There was one small bedroom downstairs that my parents and I shared. I often woke up in the early morning and would peek through my crib bars and see my mother and father close to me. I felt so safe and so loved.

Growing up, my mother learned the basics of cooking and how to cook mounds of food for masses of people, but it was her mother-in-law who taught her the finer points of making food taste and smell special. Grandma Gump was a fine pastry baker and taught my mother all she knew. These two women grew very close, resulting in my mother's deep religious beliefs as well as learning to be a good cook. Just two days before she died, when Mother could still talk to us, she told my brother she was ready to go see Jesus and Grandma Gump. Nothing from her about wanting to see my dad or her own mother.

My Gump grandparents moved to New Paris and we ended up having this big house all to ourselves. In the summer, we were outside a lot. My dad farmed the rented acreage. Mother and I would take his lunch out to the field for him. He was especially fond of chocolate milk.

Mother raised chickens. I loved to gather the eggs. It was such a great surprise to reach under those soft, warm feathers of a hen and find an egg. Sometimes the hen would peck my hand. Still, it was far more fun than hunting for colored Easter eggs in the grass. Although I was fascinated with the killing of a hen for dinner, it was very disturbing to see it flop around after Mother chopped its head off spraying blood.

She dipped the dead chicken into a boiling pot of water and then began pulling out all the feathers. I will never forget the disgusting odor of wet chicken feathers. I did like watching her cut the chicken into body parts. Cleaning dirt and gravel out the gizzard was fun. You just never quite knew what surprise might lurk in there. Believe me, I never ate a gizzard!

Because Mother was raised on a small Indiana farm, she grew up knowing all about butchering pigs and cows for food during the winter months. She knew how to make butter and cottage cheese. She had been taught early in life about collecting and preserving food. Picking berries of all kinds was a particular joy for her. She learned to make jams, jellies, and cobbler from strawberries, blueberries, and black and red raspberries. Picking tree fruit was also among her favorite chores. Peaches, cherries and apples in season were canned and jammed.

When she was young, her dad buried apples, carrots, potatoes, cabbages, and other homegrown produce in pits he dug in the ground. He layered the fruits and vegetables with straw until the pit was full. Piling a mound of dirt on top was the last step to protect the produce from weather and animals. Nuts of all kinds but especially hickory and walnuts were gathered. During long winter evenings, the Fogel girls cracked the nuts and picked out the goodies to add to cakes and cookies for a special treat. They dried corn on top of the black wood burning cook stove by letting it simmer over boiling water all day. Salt, sugar and cream were added for a special flavor. They needed few food necessities from town such as tea, sugar, flour and salt.

A rag doll, an old wooden wagon, and a hand made rag ball were mother's only toys as a child. She never had a store-bought doll. The family rule for gift giving was "necessities" came first before thinking about toys; there were never enough necessities. All the years her parents lived on that farm, there was never enough money for electricity or running water.

All her life, Mother tried to squeeze the image of that poor dirt farming life out of her veins. However, to the very end of her eighty-seven years, she delighted in gathering in strawberries, blueberries and hickory nuts. She took special pride in being able to pick blueberries faster than anyone else in the family. Just two years before she died, she was making dried corn and grape jelly.

I had to help dry corn during my childhood and came to dislike the job. I had to stir it every hour for eight hours in the special pan made just for drying corn on top of a modern stove. It was my idea of drudgery. Not only the drudgery from the stirring, but from shucking the twenty four ears of corn and trying to get every little piece of stringy sticky silk off the corn with a brush. Some of the silk always ended up on the back of my neck or behind my knees. It was a frustrating job and always done on the hottest day in mid-summer.

After Grandpa and Grandma Gump moved to New Paris, we moved upstairs to sleep. I remember lying between my parents on warm summer nights waiting for the hot day to cool and Daddy would sing to Mother and me. Songs like "You Are My Sunshine" or "A Bicycle Built for Two" and "I Danced with A Lady with A Hole in Her Stocking." Lying there safe between my parents, I could smell the warm confronting smells of an Indiana summer. A soft cooling breeze would carry the sweet smell of newly cut grass and ripening wheat as well as the whispering sound of growing corn. I loved that big farmhouse with the large front porch and the cream colored barn across the road.

Sometimes, my parents and I would take a trip to Fort Wayne for shopping and to visit friends. Mother and Daddy both loved to get all dressed up and drive into "Wayne" to see a movie. They were careful about their appearances and always took pride in their looks. So, of course, they wanted me to look good too. I had strawberry blond curly hair, which Mother rolled up in rags, a process I never understood, but it worked wonders. The next morning I would have perfect long ringlets all over my head. While my parent's enjoyed a movie, I stayed at Aunt Marie's house and played with my cousins.

Mother had a black fake fur coat for special occasions like trips to movies. Usually I would be asleep when they came to Aunt Marie's to pick me up, but I remember snuggling in that coat as Mother held me on her lap for the long drive home. I could smell winter and coal burning smoke in the fur of that coat as I watched the old globe style streetlights flash pass our car windows.

Life was good and happy on that farm. Mother, with me right behind her, would run out of the house waving her apron if an airplane happened to fly over, which was almost never. We picked flowers from the garden for our table nearly every day. Lilacs and peonies were our early favorites. The tall trees in the yard were my very special joy. I would play under their protection and lie back and stare up into their heights watching the patterns of light and dark and getting lost in an imaginary world.

Very little traffic passed by on the gravel road between the house and barn. With Mother's help, I could often cross the road for the adventure of seeing the animals in the barn. There were always baby kittens and sometimes even baby pigs to pet and help feed. The couple of years we lived in that big farmhouse were such happy years for me and I think they were happy years for my parents.

Chapter 4

My father was getting restless again. So the winter of 1944-45, Daddy bought a pretty little yellow Cape Cod house on Indiana Avenue in Goshen, and we packed up and moved. We were no longer on the farm. I had a sidewalk to roller skate and ride my scooter on and I had neighbor kids to play with every day. The house was small, very small compared to the farmhouse. There was a living room, kitchen, and two bedrooms, one bathroom and there was a basement with a coal-burning furnace. If we were away from home a long time, and the fire in the furnace went out, Daddy would have to start it up again when we came home to a cold house. When coal was burned, the residue left were hard, sharp, little nuggets called cinders. Daddy, like every other man with a coal-burning furnace, spread the ciders in our driveway instead of gravel. Cinders were very bad for small bare feet!

Mother especially liked the kitchen in this little house because it faced the street and she could see what was going on in the neighborhood and keep track of me. The yard was paradise for a little girl. Two large weeping willow trees to play house under were as good, or better, as the tall old trees on the farm. I was always upset when Daddy trimmed the trees and they no longer hung all the way to the grass. The willow tree trimming wasn't all bad. The trimmings made excellent Hawaiian grass skirts when tied around my waist.

Mother had both flower and vegetable gardens. I loved helping her with them. There was a hazelnut tree at the far end of the property. Mother still canned and made all kinds of goodies for the neighbors and us. Mother and Daddy made friends easily and fit right in with neighbors.

We became very active in the City Church of the Brethren in Goshen. Both my parents sang in the choir. This church became an important part of our lives. I never missed Sunday school; it became a high point of my week. During the church service, I was allowed to sit in the front row because my parents were in the choir. I knew all the songs by heart long before I could read, "The Old Rugged Cross," "How Great Thou Art," "In the Garden," "Amazing Grace" and many others.

Church took up most of Sunday; an hour of Sunday school and an hour of worship. After that, we visited with friends in the churchyard. My family had many friends in the church. Almost every Sunday we went to someone's house for dinner or they came to our house. In the summer, large groups of families picnicked at Wawasee, Syracuse, Stone Lake or Camp Mack. Dinner was always at noon. After a long day, most Sunday evenings of my childhood were spent eating popcorn and apples or drinking cider.

The first autumn that we lived in Goshen, Mother began teaching again. I was old enough to go to kindergarten, but our neighborhood school did not offer kindergarten. So I went to school on the other side of town. To get to school I had to cross town on a city bus. My mother tied my bus money in the corner of my hanky. I never lost my bus money.

When I started first grade, Mother took me with her to her school in Dunlap. She taught third grade. My first grade classroom was right next to her classroom. When my class walked down the hall and passed her room, I'd peek in at my mother.

Daddy did not like teaching school because he did not like being confined in a building all day. The day came when Dad decided teaching was just not for him. He had tried right after college and again in Goshen. In 1945 he stopped teaching and never looked back. He much preferred being outside and in charge of his own life. He bought a gray Ford tractor and plowed gardens for the city people. He purchased a used hay bailer to pull behind his tractor and hired out to bail hay for farmers in the summer.

My daddy could do anything; after all, he could drive a tractor and even fix it when it broke. When he let me sit on his lap on the tractor, he told me how to plow a straight row. You just had to pick out a tree or post or some other object straight across from you and drive the tractor right toward that spot. That trick worked every time and it was fun helping him find objects to drive toward.

With the war and housing problems for the military, house trailers were needed at army bases. Mother had an uncle living in Detroit who worked for a trailer manufacturer. We went to visit and Dad made a deal to buy a house trailer for the wholesale price. We then drove the trailer to Fort Knox, Kentucky and sold it for a nice profit. This was not a mobile home; it was a house trailer that attached to the car with a trailer hitch. We did this trailer-selling trip several times. Not always to Fort Knox, sometimes to Florida, but always in the South during school vacations so Mother could help with the driving.

Interstate highways did not exist and motels were not yet common. With a trailer on the back of our car, we could just pull over at night and sleep in it. Two lane roads with trucks whipping by rocking the trailer were not Mother's idea of a restful night's sleep. On the trip back to Indiana without the trailer, we would stop at cabins that rented by the night. These cabins were small. One time Mother and I had to spend a night in a cabin by ourselves. Dad stayed in another cabin. There was no lock on the door, so Mother put a chair against it. During the night a very inebriated man walked into our cabin by mistake. Mother screamed bloody murder. Scared the poor man to death as he ran out apologizing all over himself. The chair was no help at all.

So this was our new life in the "city." Mother continued to teach school during the winter. In summertime, we took trips south to sell house trailers, garden plowing in early spring and hay bailing when needed. Our social life revolved around the church and a few close neighbors. Family was always important with visiting back and forth in New Paris, just a few miles away and back to the Fogel farm between the small villages of Churubusco and Huntertown.

Life seemed good. I had everything a child could want in 1945, a happy loving family, good friends to play with and many cousins with whom to enjoy holidays. I have a picture of my fifth birthday party. My friends and I are shown all formally lined up on our front steps with our party hats on. The girls all wore dresses. I was given a white kitten for my birthday. Her name was Snowball. She stayed only a couple of days and then ran away.

I have some special memories of Daddy at the house on Indiana Avenue. He sat with me on the front steps and watched the cars go by down on the much busier Pike Street, three houses away. He would tell me the names of the cars and with each passing car; he would quiz me about what kind it was. Sometimes we had to wait several minutes in between cars. Hard to believe there was so little traffic and so few car models. There were Fords, Chevrolets, Buicks, Oldsmobiles and a few others.

In winter, Daddy would take me sledding. There was a short street with a high hill near West Goshen School. The people living on that street closed it off so kids could go sledding down that hill. Nothing was as exciting as sledding for a five-year-old kid.

Daddy also knew lots of the star constellations and would point them out to me after dark. In the evenings, we would catch lightning bugs and put them in a jar with some grass.

What amazed me as a young child, and still does, is that Daddy could recite the entire James Whitcomb Riley poem, "Little Orphan Annie," as well as parts of "The Raggedy Man" and others. He taught me the names of trees and birds and how to tell a bird by its song. He built a wren house and hung it in a tree outside my bedroom so I could hear its lovely song. He played Tidally Winks with me on the floor at night. But my all time favorite thing to do with Daddy was when he would give me flip-flops. With my back to him, I would sit on his hands and put my hands between my legs into his hands. He would pick me up that way and flip me over so I landed with my feet on the floor. I could do that for hours.

Chapter 5

I was six years old in 1946 and my parents had been married for eight years. The morning before Thanksgiving Day, Mother was up early taking the bobby pins out of her hair and getting ready for school. I didn't feel good. She took my temperature with the cold glass thermometer with the silver stuff in the bottom. She told me I had a little fever and I couldn't go to school. Mother took me across the street to Fern's house where I spent the day while Mother worked.

I slept a lot that day on Fern's couch and didn't eat much lunch. But I did color and play with blocks for a while with her little boy Jackie. The day was dark and cold. After school Mother walked over to get me. On the way home, I kept stumbling and tripping. Mom had to take my arm to keep me from falling. I was telling her about what I had done during the day and she kept asking me to repeat what I was saying to her. Years later, I learned I was mumbling my words and she could not understand me.

At home, Mother again took my temperature and made me lie down on the davenport (as we called it). She asked me what I was hungry for. Potato soup was an all time favorite cold weather comfort food and that is what I asked for. I must have slept because next thing I remember, Daddy helped me walk to the kitchen table. Daddy said grace and they started to eat. It seemed like my head was too heavy and wanted to fall backward and I was too tired to pick up my spoon. Next thing I knew Mother moved her chair next to mine and she had her hand on the back of my head holding it up to feed me with her other hand. I didn't think that was strange. I didn't care. I just wanted to lie down.

Mother and Daddy talked about what was wrong with me while we were seated at the table. Mother said Uncle Andy had told her it was a sure sign of infantile paralysis when a child could not touch their chin to their chest. Both of my parents looked at me and asked me to touch my chin to my chest. I didn't have enough control of my head to be able to do that. Now I knew something was wrong. Mother jumped up and went to the phone and started calling doctors. Daddy put me back on the davenport.

Infantile paralysis or polio was the "AIDS" of the 40's and 50's. The difference is it attacked children and occasionally young adults. It was a summertime disease and by fall families began to relax if their children were still untouched. Polio is a virus that attacks the spinal cord. Like most viruses there are high fevers and upset stomach as well as just plain sick feeling. Every case is different; it just depended on how long the virus was in the body and how many nerves it destroyed or damaged in the spinal cord. If the damage was low, you had paralysis in your legs. Higher up would affect the arms and so on.

There are three types of polio. One is a light case similar to flu and many that had this never knew it was polio. Then there is paralytic and the bulbar types. If you had paralytic polio, you experienced some paralysis in some part of your body, but you lived. Many with this kind could even "pass" as normal. Bulbar polio was deadly because it attacked the upper spine or brain stem. Few lived from this kind of polio because it attacked the nerves of muscles that controlled the diaphragm and thus breathing.

My memories of that evening are dream like. There were many people in and out of the house; my Gump grandparents, friends from church, neighbors. Friends told friends and news spread fast. All brought food because that is what people did in those days. Some people dropped off food at the door but would not come in because they did not want to infect their children. I remember someone brought a log house made of pretzels filled with cookies, cupcakes and doughnuts. The pretzel house sat on a large piece of cardboard and was put on our coffee table right in front of me. I could see in the windows the cookies and doughnuts. They looked so yummy. I hoped Mom wouldn't let all these people eat up these goodies before I felt better.

I was weak. I just lay on the davenport and watched. The doctors took me into the bedroom to check me out. It was quiet in there. My parents looked really worried. After all the poking and listening to me, the two doctors stood up. They talked to Mother and Daddy very quietly. I couldn't hear and didn't care. One doctor left and Mom walked out to the living room to call Aunt Marie in Fort Wayne.

Our family doctor agreed with Mother that it looked like I had polio and should be taken immediately to the hospital. The Goshen Hospital at this time was a converted large house, not an up-to-date modern facility. Mother and Daddy decided I should be taken to Fort Wayne. Aunt Marie was a nurse in Fort Wayne. She was able to make arrangements for a doctor to be waiting for me at St. Joseph Hospital and to get admitted late at night. St. Joseph was the same hospital where I was born. Going to Fort Wayne was a major decision to make in 1946. Long distance phone calls were very expensive and only made in dire situations.

Fort Wayne was well over an hour drive away from Goshen. I was wrapped in layers of blankets to keep warm, as car heaters were poor at best. I was laid on the back seat and Dad drove as fast as possible while Mother sat backward in the front seat to keep an eye on me. It was very late by now and there was no traffic. I remember the car going very fast over many bumps and around sharp curves.

I was not scared. I wasn't old enough to be scared. Only good things happened to me. I didn't know children could go through the valley of death. I didn't know enough to be scared. My mommy and my daddy were with me and they were praying to God that I would get better. I believed God could do anything. I was not worried.

In Fort Wayne, Dad parked the car on Wayne Street just steps from a small side door. He carried me the few steps from the car to the door. Someone inside was waiting and held the door open. They took me and put me on a stretcher. Lights, bright lights, white sheets, shots and more shots in my fanny, voices, moving people all around and then it was Thanksgiving Day and I could smell mashed potatoes and the nurse said I couldn't have any.

Happenings of the next few days are not clear to me. Someone was always taking my temperature or giving me a shot. No one ever turned the lights off. Always someone was walking around the room checking on me. Bedpans were a new revelation. I don't remember seeing Mother or Daddy for awhile. They were not allowed into the room the first few days. Some time passed, maybe a couple of days, before I was put in an iron lung. The iron lung was donated for my use by the Fort Wayne Fire Department. An iron lung is a cylinder about the size of a compact car. My body, except for my head, was placed inside and the bellows contraption underneath pulled the air in and out breathing for me. By this time, I was completely paralyzed. My eyes didn't even completely close. My arms were crossed over my chest so one hand held the other. Nothing hurt. I slept endless hours. I had both paralytic and bulbar polio.

My parents were finally allowed to see me and very seldom left my side. Nearly sixty years later, as a parent myself, I marvel that they survived those terrible days. There were endless days of terror for them. I didn't know nor care what was happening. They were adults and understood they were close to losing their only child. On six different occasions, they were told I would not live. Once while in the iron lung, they were told I was dead and a funeral home would be called in the morning to come for my body. However, no one turned off the iron lung and with my parents weeping near by, I asked for a drink of water.

All our friends back in Goshen and all our family prayed for me to live during those eighteen days I spent in the iron lung. Then I began improving enough to breathe on my own. How lucky I was! All those prayers worked for me. Thousands of children died in iron lungs. Many more children died because they were in small towns and rural communities and did not have access to or could not afford the iron lung.

My parents were told I would be in the hospital an extended period of time. Mother quit her teaching job and found a place to stay in Fort Wayne. Polio was a parent's worse nightmare; therefore my mother could not stay with anyone who had children. It was decided Mother would stay at Ray and Marguerite Swinford's house. Mother and Marguerite had been college friends and they had kept in touch over the years. The Swinfords never had any children and they lived close to the hospital. With a place to stay, Daddy went back to Goshen during the week and got a job. March of Dimes picked up my expenses, which was a great blessing.

Meanwhile I was fighting to live. Sister Kenny hot pack treatments were begun after I was released from the iron lung. The hot packs were to loosen my muscles and make them easier to move so physical therapy could begin. I still could not move any of my muscles without help. While in the iron lung, a nurse wrapped a cloth around my arms and pinned them down closer to my sides a little farther apart each day. If they had not been pinned, they would have returned to the original position on my chest. The hot packs were not fun. Nurses brought in a round shiny tub on wheels. It had boiling water in it and pieces of wool. A piece of dry wool was wrapped around one of my legs or arms. A boiling hot piece of wool followed and on top of that came a piece of plastic. This arrangement was left on until it started to cool and this process was repeated twice daily. I don't remember it being painful, but I do know I did not like seeing that tub of boiling water coming into my room. The odor of hot wet wool is still an unpleasant smell. Along with the hot pack treatments, the nurses started me on some very light exercising therapy. A nurse would simply bend my knees and elbows or at least try to without me screaming.

Christmas came. Mother gave me a doll. I named her Rose Bud. By now I was in a regular hospital bed flat on my back. I began to move my arms. If I wanted to turn my head, I would grab a hold of my hair and pull my head the way I wanted it to go. Moving anything connected to my body hurt. The first day I was forced to sit up was torture. The goal was to sit up so I could see out the window. Uncle Arlo's insurance office was across the street and I was trying to see it. With a nurse on each side of me, they gently sat me up for just a couple of minutes. It was terribly painful, but I felt such a sense of accomplishment.

There were complications along the way. I might have been out of the iron lung but I still had breathing problems. My lungs would fill with phlegm and I would be unable to breathe. Nurses would bring a long suction tube and insert it down my throat to suck out all the nastiness. Once, I clearly remembered the nurse yelling that it was not working and I was turning black. Twice I had to be taken to the operating room and have my lungs suctioned out by a doctor. The first time was at night and it was treated as a special event. Aunt Marie was there to hold my hand. The entire operating room was surrounded by Fort Wayne firefighters. They cared a great deal about children with polio and took an interest in the entire process. The doctor used a thinner but longer tube to suction my lungs.

The second time, I was wheeled into the operating room to have my lungs suctioned; I was moved from the stretcher to the operating table and strapped down. I remember thinking, "Don't they know I'm paralyzed? They are silly to strap me down." And I told my friends later about how silly that doctor was to strap down a paralyzed kid. Just where did he think I was going?

Eventually it was known I was not going to die, but I would be badly handicapped. Two nurses were assigned to me for twenty four-hour care. Miss Yost was the nurse I came to care for a lot. My doctor from the very beginning was Dr. McArdle who took exceptional care of me. I was moved to the room next to the Catholic sister's apartment on that floor. I was not Catholic and didn't know a lot about nuns. I did understand in this hospital they were on their knees praying for me.

For children who lived, bulbar polio left the face muscles weakened and distorted. My face muscles were so weak on the right side that my smile was one sided. A Sister brought me bubble gum to chew as exercise for my face. They fed me Jell-O cubes because Jell-O went down my throat easily. The bubble gum and Jell-O were special, but my face muscles did not strengthen and my smile was forever crooked.

I received many cards and well wishes from friends and family at home. I still have many of those cards. Flowers and teddy bears and other gifts came for me. Grandma Fogel often came into "Wayne" to see me. She always brought me some special food she made. I felt special and had no idea how sick I was or how my life was changed forever.

When I was able to sit in a wheelchair, I was taken down to the hospital basement and did exercises in a stainless pool of warm water. Oh, that felt so good. I enjoyed those trips to the pool, but didn't like physical exercising out of the water. Exercises out of warm water were very painful.

It took until spring before I was well enough to go home. I still could not walk, but I was improving with all the exercises. Arrangements began for me to return home. Rehabilitation classes were set up for me in Elkhart. My parents hired Miss Yost to go home with us and care for me until Mother felt comfortable with my care alone. It took awhile for all these plans to come together. In the meantime, I chewed bubble gum and did my exercises.

Grandma and Grandpa Fogel stopped in to visit me one morning. Grandma had food from the farm in the car. She was going to Aunt Marie's house to cook chicken and noodles for me and bring it back later in the day. On the way to Aunt Marie's house, a truck hit Grandpa's car. He was fine, but Grandma was banged up. She had a broken index finger, a badly broken leg and many bruises. She was now a patient with me in the same hospital. I was taken in my wheelchair down to her room to visit her several times. She was in traction and never again walked properly. In March, Grandma Fogel was still in the hospital, but I was released to go home.

Chapter 6

I was very upset that my Grandma Fogel was seriously injured and hospitalized and her life forever altered because of me. On top of that, I had to leave her in the hospital and go home all the way to Goshen. I didn't really want to go and leave her there. The last few days I was in the hospital, it became a routine for my nurse to push me in the high backed wooden wheelchair down to pool therapy and then up to see my grandma for a short visit. I could see Grandma in traction with her leg high in the air and her arm in a cast and bruises all over her face. It made me cry to see my grandma that ran like the wind lying so still.

When I was released from the hospital, my nurse, Miss Yost, came home with us back to Goshen. Miss Yost worked with me every day in the basement pool. The warm water exercise therapy was so successful the doctor told my parents to find some place at home where I could get water treatment. There were no indoor pools in Goshen. So Daddy thought he could fix anything. He made a pool in our basement. It was made of galvanized steel with high sides and had to be filled by carrying down buckets of warm water from the kitchen. There was no heater and the water did not stay warm long enough for me to exercise longer than just a few minutes. Carrying me up and down the stairs became a chore after carrying all that water. The pool didn't last more than a couple of weeks.

Miss Yost slept in my little room and privacy was limited for her. So her time with us was not long. She was interested in seeing all those Amish people she had heard about and she laughed about meeting a rich one and getting married. Many Amish people lived around Goshen and elsewhere in northern Indiana. Downtown even had a special parking lot for horse and buggies. I don't think Miss Yost ever met an Amish person while living with us.

Now that we were on our own again, Mother cared for me full time. She took me twice a week to Elkhart to a physical therapist. I hated those trips. It hurt to move my legs and it made me so tired. It was agony to hang onto bars with both hands and try to stand up over and over again. Lying down on mats and trying to lift my legs or my arms just one more time over and over.

"Come on, Roxie, you can do it. Just a little higher this time." It became a torture chamber. I have long forgotten my torturer and most of what went on there.

At home, I figured it out for myself. One day I was sitting on the davenport and Mother was in the kitchen. I wanted my doll, Rose Bud, who was over in another chair. By now I could stand up if I was hanging on to something. I slid off the davenport and hung onto the furniture. I took baby steps very slowly with rests stops in-between until I reached Rose Bud. I grabbed her and slowly slid down to the floor.

Daddy always said, "Where there is a will there's a way."

After I knew I could walk, nothing would stop me. I was like a baby learning how to walk all over again. I left the hospital in March and by warm weather in May I was outside with my friends. If I could not keep up with them, they pulled me in my red wagon. I had trouble with steps and Daddy made a banister for our front steps. At other houses, I crawled up the steps. I did what I had to do.

After I was on my feet and walking again, my parents took me to see many specialized doctors. I walked on the insides of both feet and I could not lift my right foot at the ankle when walking. So it would drag and cause me to walk with a pronounced limp. My back was not straight but it caused me no problems in getting around.

The doctors decided exercises were not enough. I needed a brace on my right foot. It was an ugly thing with metal rods that fit into my shoe on both sides and went up to just below my knee. It attached to a leather belt that buckled around my leg. This brace was to keep my foot up so it would not drag. My parents' attitude was I must never be pitied. With hard work, I could become almost the same as any other six-year-old child.

I don't think I saw things as different when I came home from the hospital. I just dealt with it. I was not a whiny kid before polio and wasn't one after. I remembered thinking *I wish I was taller and thinner,* but I never remember wishing I never had polio. Someone greater than I am will have to explain that one.

Chapter 7

*A*t that point in my life, I never heard my parents fight. If they argued, it was not when I was around. I was told many times that what was said and done in our house was not to be told to other people. Our business was our family business and not to be shared with the entire neighborhood. Daddy was paid in cash for his bailing hay and plowing garden jobs. Sometimes he counted the money and stacked it in the middle of their bed as I watched. Again, I was being told I was never to tell about this money.

I started to learn about money myself as I started losing my teeth. I would wiggle the loose tooth back and forth for weeks. When Dad reached his limit of watching me wiggle it, he would go get his pliers and pull it out. Didn't take me long to learn how to pull it before the pliers showed up. Every tooth went under my pillow with the wish for a baby sister or brother. The following morning I'd find a tiny pink rubber doll and a dime. I ended up with quite a collection of the dolls. I bought Little Lulu comics with the dimes.

Dad was getting restless. His excuse was I needed to be outside and not inside for the winter. Mother was not teaching in order to care for me so there was no reason to stay in Indiana for the winter. This time we went to Detroit and bought a trailer for ourselves and headed to California.

On the way we would stop at places and stay for a while. Dad would get a job for a week or two. I remember staying in Phoenix. The trailer was parked in a trailer court and I played in a big sandbox usually by myself. There were really tall palm trees and it was warm all the time. A blind man lived in that trailer court. He showed me how he could read with his fingers. Since Mother was "home schooling" me and I was learning to read, I thought it was really amazing how he could read not using his eyes. I missed nearly the entire first grade, so mother decided to teach me and catch me up. We didn't stay any place long enough for me to go to school.

We made it to California and settled down in the Santa Ana area. In this trailer park there were some kids I played with. There was a stone drive around the park and I had trouble walking on all those stones. I fell many times and I'm sure I still have pieces of those little stones, as well as cinders from our drive at home, embedded in my knees to this day. Dad was not home much. He got a job someplace because there was no other money coming our way.

One day we moved to a farm called a "ranch" in California. It was a pig ranch and Dad was the manager. We parked the trailer next to the office and we lived in the little house. And this was a really little house. The kitchen was small, the living room was pretty big but there was just one bedroom. I slept on the sofa. Sleeping on that couch is how I learned the truth about Santa Claus.

The pig ranch was great fun. If I stood on top of one of the pig houses, I could see the Pacific Ocean. There were two rows of pens for the pigs to live in with a drive running between these two rows. All of this was fenced in. A Mexican man worked on the ranch with my dad. His name was Manuel and he was very nice. He brought me a puppy, but it had to sleep in the barn. Garbage trucks from Santa Anna came out and dumped their garbage in the drive between the pigpens. I would stand on a rail of the fence and watch Manuel and Dad rake through the garbage for items that could be harmful to the pigs. What fun that was to me. They found all sorts of stuff. Once they found a one hundred-dollar bill. Usually they found kitchen items like knives, silverware and dishes and even whole turkeys and chickens. Linen napkins and table cloths were common finds. Mother kept one of the big butcher knives the rest of her life.

The house was not as exciting as the pig pens. There were no closets and no chest of drawers; however, there were a few pieces of furniture.

Daddy got some wooden orange crates that Mother stacked up and used for storing our clothes.

Around the front of the house was a hedge taller than I was and it was all geraniums. I still like the smell of geraniums. I hid in that hedge when I saw and heard my first helicopter. It flew over our house and I had no idea what it was.

There were poinsettias behind the house that grew taller than the house. Mother had a garden in the side yard. All I remember growing there were carnations.

Daddy decided my brace was not helping me at all and he cut it off. The brace was meant to keep my right foot up so it didn't drag, but it seemed I went too fast and was always tripping and falling. Whenever I fell I needed something near by, like a chair, to use to pull myself up. If I fell in an open area, I had to yell for help. Daddy was tired of coming to my rescue several times a day, so he cut off the brace. I was delighted to have that hot heavy thing gone. Now I could move even faster and I fell less. I learned to pick that leg up higher and went on my way. And when I did fall, it seemed easier to get up by myself without a brace holding me down.

I was really enjoying my stay in California. Grandma and Grandpa Gump came to see us for Christmas. I don't really remember how they got there, but it makes sense to me that they came by train since Grandpa had worked for the railroad. Mother and I went shopping in Santa Ana for Christmas gifts and I watched Santa arrive by parachute. "Here Comes Santa Claus" by Gene Autry, was the hit song that Christmas season of 1947. The only snow was on top of a mountain called Old Baldly. Daddy took us up to the top one hot day and we threw snowballs at each other.

During my grandparents' stay, we had several picnics at the beach. Everywhere new buildings were going up, but the beach was open for all. We would spread out our blankets and sit on them while Grandpa Gump stood to say grace. Now when he said grace it could take several minutes and I kept my eye on those waves rolling in toward us. I was sure he wouldn't say Amen in time to run for higher ground.

Grandpa and Grandma Gump slept in our house trailer parked behind the house. They came into the house for meals and spent most of their time with us. Christmas was the usual turkey dinner with all the trimmings. Grandma made pies like only she could. It was a good holiday. I had come far since the Christmas before in St. Joseph Hospital.

We took some time to visit and explore other parts of California while Grandpa and Grandma Gump were with us. We visited San Francisco and the huge redwood trees of Northern California. Children remember differently than adults, of course, and I'm certain my parents and grandparents remembered that trip for the natural beauty of God's creations in that area. I remember a park we visited. The picnic basket was full and heavy so we left it sitting on a picnic table and went off to see the park. There were some cages with animals and other interesting sights to see. The acorns from the oak trees were long instead of round like in Indiana. When we returned to our table, the picnic basket lid was open and a cat was inside eating our hot dogs. Another cat was under the table chewing on a hot dog. In Indiana, raccoons would have been in the basket. Left undaunted, we ate what was left in our picnic basket and had a grand day.

I don't know how long Grandpa and Grandma Gump stayed with us and I don't remember attending church, but I know we did. The day did come when my Grandparents returned to New Paris and we were alone again.

We stayed only a few months on the pig ranch and then the day came when we packed our few belongings back into the trailer. I had to say good-by to Manuel and gave him back my dog. I was sad to go and I watched the buildings slide past as we drove down the lane onto other adventures.

We were going back to Indiana, but taking the long way home. We stopped and visited the newly-built Hoover Dam and the home of Will Rogers. As I remember, it was someplace in Nevada where we stayed a few days in a trailer park. Mother and I would walk down the hot, dusty street to the nearest store for groceries. I didn't notice any trees. While at that same trailer park, Daddy decided we should sell the trailer and he did. We packed all of our belonging into the car.

Chapter 8

$\mathcal{S}$ometime in the spring of 1948 we arrived back on Indiana Avenue in Goshen, Indiana. We'd been gone about eight months. I started back at West Goshen Elementary. I was in a regular first grade classroom. I stayed in that school through the second grade. I was no longer the average first grader, I was the crippled kid. Some students who didn't know me stopped and stared and made fun of the way I walked and smiled.

Goshen was small enough that every time you went to the grocery store, five-and-dime or hardware, you met someone you knew. And yet, Goshen was big enough where there were lots of people you didn't know. Goshen was truly an all American town, a safe home and community with freedom. I was so lucky to have grown up in Goshen in the forties and fifties.

The only restaurant I remember in town was Stiemans on Main Street. There were ice cream shops like South Side Soda Shop, or the bus stop downtown at the Olympia and there were drug stores where you could get a sandwich wrapped in greasy waxed paper and a cherry coke. During the summer time the only theater in town had movies just for kids on Saturday afternoons. Mother would give me money for a SloPoke sucker and it would last the entire movie. After the show was over, I would go next door to the drug store and call Mom to come get me. Of course, I had a coke or an ice cream soda while waiting for her. Margaret O'Brien was my favorite actress and I loved all the Lassie movies.

We attended movies as a family sometimes in the evenings. Often those shows scared me to the point where I would hide my face and not look at the screen. I bit my fingernails and Mom gave me clay to play with during movies so I wouldn't bite my nails.

We never told the Gumps about going to the movies or about playing cards. Mom and Dad loved to play pinochle and had card parties weekly at one friend's house or another. Mother wore shorts but she kept a skirt near by if my grandparents stopped in. Grandma Gump was such a kind person, she never would have said anything. Mother just didn't want to be disrespectful.

Sometimes on Saturday night, we would drive downtown and vertical park on Main Street like normal, except we weren't shopping because most of the stores were closed. We would get out of the car to visit with people we knew walking by. It didn't take long until there would be several entire families just standing around talking. Sometimes we walked along with friends until we found other friends to stop and chat with. Everyone felt completely safe and happy.

Attending school was fun even though I was far from being a great student. I was self-conscious because I was the odd one. Most of my neighborhood friends were in this same school.   We sat in circles for reading and stood when it was our turn. I hated standing up in front of everyone; I could hear the whispers behind me. This common practice went on through elementary school and in Sunday school. It never got easier for me, until I was an adult.

Mother was not teaching. I still needed special care. She decided to stay home with me. It was a long time before she returned to teaching. She spent her time with household chores. It took an entire day to do the laundry. Mother had a wringer washing machine. After the laundry was washed, everything was hung outside to dry. Then everything had to be ironed and ironing took most of another day.

The main meal of the day was supper in the evening. We seldom ate "fresh" vegetables, no fresh salads like I eat today. Fresh fruits and vegetables were eaten only in season; otherwise, we ate canned produce. We ate many cooked vegetables and Jell-O fruit salads with a spoon full of mayonnaise on top. Fruits were often cooked in cobblers. Meat was the main part of the meal. Pork chops, ham, Swiss steak and gravy, fried chicken were favorite foods. Nobody thought much about diet and there were no spicy foods like pizza or tacos.

Mother also spent a lot of her time doing things for the church. She also spent time with her friends. Not many ladies worked away from home so there were plenty of friends around. They gave each other home permanent waves made by Toni and discussed whether *Parent's Magazine* said the new movie in town was okay for kids to see.

We visited Grandpa and Grandma Gump in New Paris every week or so. I liked going to church with Grandma Gump. She always had something in her purse for me to eat. She would fold and roll her handkerchief into a baby cradle for me to play with. We went to church every Sunday morning and Sunday evening with prayer service on Wednesday evening. We didn't go to many of the evening services unless we were in New Paris. Grandpa Gump would preach so we had to go.

Once in awhile I stayed overnight at Grandma Gump's. Grandma would take all her teeth out and she put them in a glass of water on the dresser at night. I thought that was amazing.

Grandma Gump was as close to perfect as you can get on earth. She never spoke ill of anyone. Just the opposite, speaking only of the good she saw in people. She was always helping others and giving whatever she could whether it was food, clothing, time or prayers. She belonged to the ladies aid society at church and she made quilts for other people. I never saw her angry or upset. Plus all those virtues, her pie crust was out of this world. I sat in the back seat of our car many times on homeward bound trips over hearing my parents comparing the pie crusts of my two grandmothers. Fogel never came close.

I never knew much about Grandma Gump's childhood, except for the story she told me. When she was a little girl her family lived in a log cabin just east of Churubusco, Indiana. During warm weather, the family hung a deerskin for the door. Every evening about supper time a hand would appear around that deerskin. They would put food on the hand and it would go away. The hand belonged to an Indian. I loved that story.

Chapter 9

$\mathcal{D}$addy was on the go again. This time we didn't go far. He bought a farm on Main Street on the northern edge of Goshen. The house was within city limits and the barn was in the county. So we left the pretty little house on Indiana Avenue with the weeping willow trees and moved into a huge, cold farmhouse. Just the three of us rattled around in this large old house. I left my friends and my school where I had felt safe.

I started third grade at Chamberlain School. I didn't know anyone and was once again the odd duck. I remember drinking the cold fountain water and it hurt my teeth. Teeth were important because we placed gold stars on a chart if we brushed our teeth before coming to school every morning.

Daddy did some farming on North Main Street. He raised chickens in the barn. But the real income came from the house. Inside the front door, there was a nice-sized vestibule and beyond that was a very large room, which we never used as a family. This big front room became a commercial dining room. Beyond it was a smaller room, which was our living room. Next was the kitchen that had a large walk-in pantry with numerous shelves and storage bins. On a small back porch there was the large deep freeze.

Mother, never one to sit still, turned this house into a restaurant. She named it "The Country Kitchen." She served dinners on Friday and Saturday evenings and Sunday afternoons, and only by reservation. The menu was always the same; fried chicken, swiss steak or ham. Vegetables varied and the desserts changed. There was always mashed potatoes with gravy and homemade rolls and jam. Since restaurants were not nearly as common as now, Mother had a good business. A lot of private holiday parties and family celebrations booked far in advance.

Mother hired a lady to help serve. If she was sick and could not work or if more help was needed, Aunt Blanche helped. This was great fun for me. We had a commercial business license and could go to the Wray Ice Cream factory in Elkhart and buy large quantities of ice cream, a gallon of each flavor. More often than not, we bought several gallons of coconut pineapple and black cherry because they were big favorites with our paying guests as well as the three of us. We needed that big deep freeze on the back porch to hold all the ice cream. During most of the week the dining room was empty and I was allowed to play in that room.

There were drawbacks to this kind of business. The kitchen and family living space was a mad house on nights we served guests. The staircase to our bedrooms was in the big dining room, so I had to pass by some of the guests on my way to bed. Thank God, it was not an open staircase so diners could not see me struggle up the stairs.

Mother was exhausted the rest of the week. Dad helped out with the business. Delivery trucks needed unloading and he helped with carrying heavy things to and from the pantry. During the week, Mom cleaned and did other household chores. I helped with the family dishes. There was no automatic dishwasher. There were many dishes to be hand washed after a dinner in the dining room. Dad even washed a dish or two. It was in this house that I saw him actually iron something. He decided the iron was no good (Mom complained about that iron for weeks) and went out and bought a new one.

Someone gave me a really nice mutt named Rags. This older dog followed me all around. Someplace I also acquired two puppies. They were part collie and I loved them dearly. The friendly one was black and white. The shyer one was tan and white. My dogs were never allowed in the house. They slept in one of the sheds, but had the run of the farm during the day. A delivery truck pulled into the driveway one morning and after it left, when I was in the bathroom on the toilet, Daddy came in, squatted down in front of me and told me the delivery truck ran over the tan puppy and it was dead. So Daddy explained how he took Rags and Blackie behind the shed and shot them because they would be too lonely without their friend. Something turned over in me that day. I was the crippled kid, the pitied kid, the fat kid and the mimicked kid for nearly two years and now, added to that burden, I lost trust in my daddy.

During this year I had been taken to doctors to see if I could be helped. Someone suggested I had sinus problems and I spent time every evening sitting under an ultra blue light. It smelled funny, like what I now think of as ozone. I wore special goggles to protect my eyes. This stopped when Mother got tired of it, but it did go on most of the winter. Dad was gone for a short time when we lived here. I think it was a trip for something to do with the church. I remember talking to him on the phone and eating an orange.

My parents still had many friends, but their social lives slowed down because the Country Kitchen took all their time and energy, especially on weekends. Both Mother and Dad lived by the principles of "Don't put off until tomorrow what you can do today," "A penny saved is a penny earned" and "A job worth doing is a job worth doing well." I was also expected to live by those axioms and was told so daily.

By the summer of 1949 we were traveling again. This time we were going with Grandpa and Grandma Gump, Uncle Arlo, Aunt Dorothy and their daughters, Marilyn and Lois to the Church of the Brethren National Conference in Ocean Grove, New Jersey. Not only did we go to the conference; we went to New York City. There we visited China Town, the Empire State Building and the Statue of Liberty. It was very exciting.

The church conference was boring! It was like church every day all day. But where we stayed was another story indeed. Ocean Grove was on the Atlantic Ocean with a boardwalk and all the trimmings. The church had made housing available for those who needed it in summer "cottages." Now these were not what I had known as cottages. These were Victorian

summer apartment houses. Big porches included. There were two long
rows of cottages situated vertically to the boardwalk with probably twenty-five houses in each row. In between cottages was a park area with grass,
flowers and trees. Several families stayed in each house. Each family had
their own apartment, which consisted only of bedrooms and a bath. We did
not eat in the apartment. There were special places where we went for
meals. Of the meals, all I remember is standing in line and Dad always having pie a la mode or apple pie with a slice of cheese on it. He also liked cottage cheese sprinkled with brown sugar.

We were at the conference a week that summer. Mother took
Marilyn and me to the beach as often as possible. We were very fair
skinned and I got terribly sunburned on my back. In the evenings, we often
walked along the boardwalk. Dad took me to the amusement park and put
me on a pony for a ride on the merry-go-round. I had never ridden alone
before. If you could get the brass ring, you got a free ride. Dad was yelling
at me to get the ring and it was way out of my reach, of course. The ride
stopped and Dad did not get me down and I could not get down by myself.
When the ride started again and the man came around for tickets, I didn't
have one. I was petrified with shame. I broke a rule and the man running
the ride was mad at me. I couldn't believe Dad let this happen. At the end
of that ride, Dad helped me down. When questioned, he said all the other
kids were staying on for two rides without tickets. No big deal to him. It
was a big deal to me. I had to please people to make them like me, and
heaven forbid, never draw attention. These were the lessons I learned in
life and now Dad just caused someone to be upset with me.

Finally the conference was over and we were going home by way
of Philadelphia. We stopped to see the Liberty Bell and all the buildings
around it. Then Dad decided I needed to see skid row. He drove around
until he found it and I got to see drunks lying in the street. Dad kept repeat-
ing, "How could this be happening in the City of Brotherly Love?"

Goshen looked good when we returned to North Main Street. And even though I didn't like this house, I was home. I was not yet nine and I had been from coast to coast. I'd been to Canada and Mexico. And I had been near death. My nature was to be optimistic. I still always tried to find what's good in any situation. Mother was the same. Every time we reentered Indiana from wherever we had been, she sang, "Back Home Again in Indiana." We took up life where we left off and life would continue just the same, or so I thought.

Chapter 10

other used to tell me that God had special blessings for me because I was crippled. I never quite understood, but I didn't argue. It was a comforting thought. My parents never babied me anyway. I was expected to live life as normally as possible. I slowly became a lonely child. We moved around so much that I didn't have time to make long lasting friendships. No playmates lived near the pig farm the months we spent in California. Moving to North Main Street, I lost all my neighborhood friends. There were still church friends and I still went to church-related functions, but I was alone more and more. Mother tried to keep me busy and read to me every evening. But she had a lot to do for The Country Kitchen. My favorite playthings were paper dolls. I spent hours cutting out the entire wardrobes for my collection of cardboard dolls. These were not baby dolls. They were made to look like movie stars and had very elaborate clothing. Every piece of paper clothing had several little white tabs to fold over in order to attach the clothing to the doll. It was very tedious work. But when all was ready, I could play with my paper friends and make intricate stories about each one.

Sometime while we were traveling around the West, Grandpa and Grandma Fogel moved. Uncle Andy bought a farm just on the northern edge of Huntertown and my grandparents moved there. I liked this house because of the big trees in the front yard. They were maples with huge yellow leaves in the fall. This house had plumbing and a heating system, but Grandma still kept a chamber pot under her bed for as long as she lived there.

Every summer after they moved to Huntertown, I spent a week at Grandma Fogel's farm. Usually my cousin Delno and I were there together. He became one of my closest cousins. We had such fun playing in the barn and following Grandpa around. Grandma Fogel had us gather eggs and help wash them and put them in a crate. She sold the eggs and that money was hers to keep, so she hid it from Grandpa.

I had to lie down and rest every afternoon. The room I was in had a door that opened unto the sun porch. Del would sit out there and read *Life* magazine while waiting for me to get up. He would hold up pictures for me to see and we would laugh about them. Then he began to find twenty-dollar bills in the magazines. We went through several magazines in a big stack on the porch and found several twenty-dollar bills. We were careful to put them back in exactly the same place.

Toward the end of that week, Grandpa Fogel took me into Fort Wayne to spend a couple of days with my cousins Kay and Carol. My cousin Carol was a teenager. Kay and I didn't see much of Carol, except if she needed something. She would send us to the Rexall Drug Store at the corner of Anthony and Lake for Noxema. Carol would have to write it down because we would forget and we couldn't pronounce it. We bought movie magazines for ourselves.

When I returned to the farm, Del couldn't wait to tell me Grandma Fogel had burned all the magazines. We worried about those twenty-dollar bills, but we never found out what happened to them. Knowing Grandma Fogel, she did not burn them. I later learned she not only hid money in magazines, she also hid money in the hems of curtains.

Whenever I stayed at the farm, I slept with Grandma Fogel. Grandpa Fogel slept in the other room. Grandma would whisper in my ear how bad the Catholics were and I was to be careful and never marry one. Catholics hid guns in their basements and you had to sign your children over to the church. She also warned me never to talk to strangers, but was vague about why it was dangerous.

Yet when she took me with her to "Wayne," she didn't follow her own rules. She always stopped for tea and doughnuts at Murphy's coffee shop. Before going in the revolving door, she again would warn me not to talk to strangers. Once seated at the counter, she talked to everyone seated or working at the counter. Before we left she knew the life history of everyone present and just how they might possibly be related to her, or someone she knew.

Appearances were everything to Grandma Fogel. She did not leave the house without a hat, gloves and purse. It was important to always act and look like a lady. One time, Kay and I had played house upstairs and moved the window curtains just a little. When Grandma came back from the grocery store and saw that crooked curtain, she was angry. She was sure the neighbors discussed her lack of housekeeping skills just because of that curtain. It is strange how a small childhood incident can follow you all your life. As an adult woman with a home of my own, every morning as I raise my bedroom shades, I make sure they are straight.

Grandma knew everyone in town and everything there was to know about him or her. This was not being nosy. She cared about the people near her and was there to help in times of trouble. Before her car accident on the way to hospital to see me, she had been a tall thin woman who walked very fast. After that accident, she wore a built up shoe and never walked fast again.

These trips to the farm were just what I needed. Right after sunset, before it became dark, I liked to sit on the front steps under the big trees and watch the birds all lined up on the telephone wires. They seemed to chat back and forth always change their seating arrangements. It was God's world working in peace and calm quietness after a day of hot busy labors.

Most summers, we also spent some time at a lake in northern Indiana lake country. Once or twice we went to Canada and stayed in a cabin. This was usually a fishing vacation. But the summer after we returned from New Jersey, change was again in the air. This time it was a very big change.

My parents had felt what they thought was God's calling while in Ocean Grove at the church conference. Amazing! I had only felt sunburned. But their belief was that they were seriously called into the mission field and they were making plans to become missionaries in South America. First step, they needed more specialized education in the areas of home economics, agriculture and, of course, Spanish. They applied and were accepted to Cornell University in Ithaca, New York. It was late summer and the beginning of school was approaching.

Life started to move in high gear. The Country Kitchen was not reopened and everything had to be sold. All those ugly green glass dishes that Martha Stewart and others want to collect in today's world, had to be sold. Tables, chairs, napkin holders, kitchen pots and pans, farm equipment and many of our personal belongings had to go. Dad decided we would have an auction. Everything we couldn't get in our car or store in Grandma Fogel's barn went out in our front yard for the sale. I was heart broken.

The auction started with a crowd of people present for the sale. I'm sure most people were just plain curious. Everything was out in the open and strangers picked over it and talked about all the objects that had made up our lives.   Garage sales or flea market did not happen in the 40's and an auction was good cheap family entertainment. Cars were parked all over the place so it was easy for me to go unnoticed. I took my time and looked over the situation. When the coast was clear, I grabbed my favorite Teddy Bear that Mother said I was too old for, and hid it in our car. I felt a little better. I had taken back a small piece of my life.

Chapter 11

$\mathcal{O}$nce everything was sold, we headed for Ithaca. Now when I think of that trip, or hear of Ithaca, New York or Cornell University TV football games, it brings to mind bright sunny fall days with the smell of burning leaves. I think of big bright yellow, orange and red leaves piled taller than my head begging to be jumped into. Most of the short time we spent in Ithaca was good.

Dad rented us an apartment. I had never lived in an apartment before and this one had two toilets! One was straight inside the front door. I think it was a converted closet because that's all that was in there, just a toilet. It was a nice apartment and it was furnished. Ithaca was not flat like Goshen. There were twenty-five steps leading up the hill to our apartment house and then a few more steps up to the door. Good thing we lived on the ground floor. It was impossible for me to get up all those steps from the street without a rail. Dad got permission to install a simple pipe railing. Now I could come and go on my own.

I just turned nine and the school year was already well underway. Mother enrolled me in school. It was a big school, because Ithaca is bigger than Goshen and I was in the fourth grade. Mother drove me to school and I walked home. I had an oval- shaped metal lunch pail that had red and white gingham design on the bottom with a red lid and two red handles. Grapes were in my lunch nearly every day for weeks. On my first day in this new school, I was shown into the room and introduced to the class. An entire room of complete strangers stared at me and watched me limp to my seat and I wanted to crawl in a hole. I sat down at an empty desk behind a black boy. It was the first time I'd been that close to a black person. There weren't black people in Goshen. When everyone settled down, the boy in front of me turned around and whispered, "I bet you're nice!" I have no idea what his name was but he was the only reason I ever went back to school again. I don't remember ever talking to each other after that first day. I don't remember anyone else from that school, except the teacher. What I remember about her is she used hand puppets when she told a story.

I had to walk home from school because Mother and Dad were in classes at the university. Until my parents came home, I stayed with two elderly ladies who lived across the street from our apartment. Their house was flush with the street and it was easy for me to get there. I don't remember their names. They were widowed sisters living together. They spoiled me with fresh warm cookies or other homemade treats when I arrived each day from school. When we left Ithaca, one of these ladies gave me a toy she had as a little child. It was two dogs holding an umbrella and they rattled if you shook them, a treasured procession to this day.

Home and school were important, but our lives revolved around the church. At one church or another was where our lives really centered while we lived in Ithaca. The first church we went to was much too big for my father's liking. Even though we were warmly welcomed, we only attended a couple of services. There were several other churches before we settled on one in the country. It was a small white wooden church with lots of trees, their leaves turning brilliant fall colors. We helped rake leaves in the church yard and made friends with the people of this church. We visited back and forth at their houses and once again, I had church friends.

Dad started being a guest preacher. One Sunday we went to a very little, very old church way out in the countryside and after a while, Dad became their full time preacher. He was still going to school but preaching didn't take up much time. Now we went to church Sunday morning, Sunday night and Wednesday night prayer meetings. A well-to-do family pretty much ran this church and they liked Dad. We were invited to Sunday dinner at their farm. Mother made sure I was clean behind the ears and everywhere else. This was not the kind of farm I had always known. I don't remember the barns, only the house. It was a mansion in my eyes. Deep carpets, drapes that touched the floor, French doors leading to a flower garden and more silverware on the table than I knew what to do with.

After some time, things did not go well at this church for Dad or me. First, I knew I had trouble reading. When I had to read unfamiliar material, like something from the Sunday school lesson, I froze. I tried to read, but I mostly stammered and wanted to disappear. Boys in the class made fun of my reading. I panicked and hated going. I never told Mother. I was ashamed and thought it was entirely my fault because I just was not good enough. The teacher was kind to me, but she could not control the boys. She never told Mother.

Meanwhile, Dad was having his own problems. Boys in their late teens began heckling him during sermons. Several times we found very large rocks behind the tires of our car when we tried to leave after church. This usually happened on Wednesday evening when it was dark outside.

My parents discovered there was a hospital for handicapped children in Ithaca. It was the Franklin D. Roosevelt Hospital and they took me to see if anything could be done to correct my crooked body. They already tried prayer healing and that didn't work. After many tests, they were told I needed more than one surgery to correct my problems. They suggested Mother and Dad rethink their lives and not leave the United States until I received the necessary surgical corrections. The surgeries needed to be completed before I stopped growing which would be around the age of sixteen.

God changed the course of our lives and decided to get us back on track, because long before Christmas I was told of a miracle. My mother was expecting my long-awaited and much longed for sister or brother. Needless to say, that ended the missionary dream and we were going back to Indiana!

Chapter 12

$\mathcal{B}$y late fall in 1949 we were back in Indiana, but not in Goshen. Dad rented a farm south of New Paris. I think the owners were gone for the winter because all their furniture was still in place. We spent the majority of our time in the large country kitchen, sitting at the big table playing Monopoly, checkers, Chinese checkers and many other board games. Mother was a great fan of jigsaw puzzles. I was very fond of playing with modeling clay and made entire towns including houses, sidewalks, trees and people. My clay village became so big, Mother made me move it into the other room.

A red barn was at the end of the drive not far behind the house. West of the house was a small apple orchard and a railroad track just west of that. Hobos still occasionally rode trains in 1949. Once in awhile a Hobo would show up at the back door and offer to pick up windfall apples, clear brush or rake leaves for food. After the work was finished, Mother would give him a big plate of food and he would sit on the back steps to eat it. Just watching him eat, I understood he really enjoyed every bite. The hobos were always polite and appreciative.

We spent Christmas of 1949 in this house. Mother was getting big. She wore maternity clothes that consisted of a skirt with an expandable front panel and over that a tent-like blouse. Mother was very careful about her appearance and sometimes polished her nails and wore "rats" in her hair to make it look fuller. This was nothing new; she always was doing her nails and setting her hair with bobby pins. She polished her nails so carefully, always letting the half moons show and leaving the very tips left unpolished. She favored bright red nail polish in those days.

One of Grandpa Fogel's sisters married George Iler. They lived in Garrett north of Fort Wayne in a big house and had money. George Iler was a Shriner and he sponsored me to the Shriner Crippled Children's Hospital in Oak Park, Illinois, a suburb of Chicago. My first physical exam at the Shriner Hospital was November 25, 1949.

Thus began a new area in our lives. My parents and I went to Chicago every three months to the clinic in the hospital. After sitting in the waiting room for hours with what seemed like hundreds of other kids and their families, I would be called for my exam by a doctor. Mother and I walked along a hallway lined with curtain covered cubicles. Each tiny cubicle contained an examining table and one chair. After another wait, a doctor came in. The doctor had me walk up and down the hall. He tapped me on the knee and ankle with his little rubber hammer just like many doctors before him. He then talked to my mother about the best treatment for me. Surgery on my feet was step one. We would just have to wait until there was an opening for me in the hospital. Until then, we were to come back in three months to check on my progress. At home, I was to lose weight and exercise more.

After we finished at the hospital, the rest of the trip to Chicago was fun. We always drove Lake Shore Drive into the city and saw the tall skyscrapers on the left side and Lake Michigan on the right. Sometimes we went to a big Sears store and went shopping. We went to the Loop and ate at the "Egg and I." Mother and Dad always made a big production of these trips to Chicago. It took about four hours to drive there and four more to drive home. No interstate highways, just two lane roads all the way to Chicago passing through multitudes of small towns and villages. We did not stay over night thus making this trip a very long day. We left home before dawn and returned home after dark.

On March 13, 1950 my sister, Zandra, was born. Mother had several friends from our Goshen church over for dinner the evening before. Mother's water broke during the dinner. She put a towel between her legs and went right on with the dinner. When the dinner guests were gone, Dad took her to the Goshen Hospital, after dropping me off at Aunt Blanche and

Uncle Ralph's house in New Paris.

Mother did not want her children to have common names. She had been a teacher long enough to know it's better not to have too many "Marys" or "Johns" in one class. So she named us unusual names. Aunt Melba suggested my name. She knew a young girl named Roxann and liked that name. The girl died of polio. Zandra's name came from one of Mother's first students. I always liked having an "X" in my name. I think Zandra always liked that her name started with a "Z."

Mother and Zandra finally came home, but, of course, life was never the same again. It had improved a little. I had a baby sister albeit she was just a wee little thing and not much fun. I did enjoy holding and feeding her the bottle. Mother said I was such a help to her. It had been many years since she had a baby and she was older and used to her own time schedule.

When Zandra was a baby, we went to Florida to visit relatives. Zandra went from being a bundle of joy to a real pain in the neck. She was a screamer. Mother would get in the car and I would hold Zandra and we would drive all over Sebring, Florida. Zandra would go to sleep when the car was moving. Sometimes we were lucky, and could get her back in her bed and she wouldn't wake up. When we returned to Goshen, the doctor gave Mother Phenobarbital to help settle Zandra down. Mother bought it in a large quart bottle. Zandra took it by the spoonful until she was three.

Chapter 13

*W*ith spring and summer coming, we had to move again. We moved before the end of the school year, so I finished the fourth grade in the third school I attended that year. Our next house was just west of Goshen on the Harry Green Road. Our house sat on two acres of land. The only problem with this house was there was only one bedroom. Zandra was still in her crib so she didn't take up much space. I had a twin bed and there was a double bed for Mother and Dad. We all slept in one bedroom.

At this house, Mother had two flower gardens. Bachelor buttons were one of her favorite flowers at that time. There were climbing roses and Grandma Gump gave her a start of Rose Moss for at the front door. I particularly enjoyed collecting Rose Moss seed. Another one of Mother's favorite flowers were Tea roses. She was forever trying to start new ones under an upside down glass jar. She also had a big vegetable garden. We had lots of space outside and Dad planted peanuts just so I could see they grew like potatoes and not on a tree like nuts.

Dad had two long chicken houses built out of cement block behind the house. In these chicken houses he raised 18,000 chickens until they were broiler market sized. When the baby chicks came from the hatchery, it was so such fun! I helped unpack the cute fuzzy little peeping chicks. High school boys or my cousins were hired to help with the work of unpacking the baby chicks because there were just too many for us to unpack in a few hours.

Dad took bales of straw and made small circular pens to keep the little peeps in until they grew a bit. We had to be very careful not to step on them and I confess I did step on one or two. Fresh straw was put down on the floor and the chicks were hard to see sometimes. The chicks drank from upside down jars of water set in pans and ate grain from big round pans.

There were several of these straw pens set up throughout both buildings.

After the chickens were settled in, Dad and his Uncle Roy built a new bedroom on to the south end of the house. The room was large enough for Zandra, still in her crib to share with our parents. Dad and Uncle Roy tried the new idea of built in closet space with sliding doors with great success.

In this house, next to the fireplace on both sides were built in book-shelves. We easily filled them to overflowing. Under the shelves were large storage chests. They were soon filled with picture albums and Zandra's toys, and maybe a few things of mine. I don't know where the furniture came from but I do remember the piano. Grandpa had a big up-right black piano that he gave to us and it was in our living room as was Dad's desk.

I finished fourth grade that spring and started fifth grade the following fall at Model School. I rode the yellow school bus back and forth to school. I really got my education on that bus. I learned about sex (not just my Mother's version) by listening around me. Of course, it turned out to be mostly wrong.

In Model School, I had friends again. I didn't play with them every day, but I did go to their houses and was invited to birthday parties. I felt good about my home and my school, but I did not feel good about myself. I was becoming very chubby. I wore Cinderella Chubbete size dresses. Mother and Dad were always on me about what I ate. Thyroid tests were done and my thyroid was fine. Nothing seemed to work. Being fat with a crooked smile, a limp when I walked, plus wearing glasses and not being able to read well-all worked together to make my life a personal nightmare. I lived with it each and every day for years. No one chooses to be fat or crippled or a poor reader, but I was all of them and I could see no way out of this mess.

Then Shriners Hospital called and there was an opening for me.

Before being taken to Chicago, my parents wanted me to be baptized. In the Brethren Church you are not baptized at birth. You are baptized when you or your parents feel you are ready, usually as a young adult.

In the basement of our church was the baptismal pool. It was a pool under a trap door in the floor. The door was lifted and you walked down a few steps into the water where the preacher met you. In my case he prepared the audience for a miracle. Maybe I would come out of the water healed and not need to go to Chicago. I was too nervous to even give a miracle a second thought. Anyway, I had learned my problems were not that easily solved.

I waited in an adjacent room listening to Reverand Fike speak. When the time was right, some ladies led me to the pool steps. All the church sat there on folded metal chairs and watched. After all, most of them had prayed for me in 1946 and I had lived. Maybe it would work again. I did not wear a Sunday dress but an everyday dress that was allowed to get wet. Down in the water, Reverand Fike put his hands on my head and prayed almost as long as Grandpa Gump.

After the prayer, I kneeled and with a cloth in his hand, Reverand Fike covered my mouth and nose. He then dunked me three times in the water in the name of the Father, the Son and the Holy Ghost. Another shorter prayer and I was baptized. Ladies met me at the top of the steps with dry blankets and I limped back to the room with every eye watching me walk. No miracle. How many miracles does one little girl get anyway?

Chapter 14

Shriners gave us just a few days notice, but it was not hard to get ready to go. All I was allowed to take was my Bible, letter writing material and my one and only pair of brown lace up shoes.

I entered the hospital the first time on Friday, October 13, 1950. I had just turned 10 years old. My parents said good bye to me in the old clinic where we had been coming for almost a year. I had to undress and give Mother my clothes. A nurse gave me hospital clothes. She then took me to the girls' ward and showed me my bed where I was to sit and wait. I did. I sat and sat and sat. No one else was anywhere around. I could see the bathroom and needed to use it. Finally, I got up the courage to get off the bed and used the bathroom.

After a very long time of waiting there all alone and scared beyond belief, girls flooded into this ward. Some were walking, some were in wheelchairs, some were on stretchers pushed by nurses and some were in cripple carts, which were a lot like wheelchairs except you laid down more than you sat up. I was in the land of the crippled. I was different only because I was new. Imagine that!

The hospital took up an entire city block. On the other side of the railroad tracks was the Mars Candy Company whose founder, Frank Mars, also had polio. The main part of the hospital was two stories. Living quarters for student nurses were on the second floor. This floor also included wings for offices and one large area for surgery. The ground floor contained the most important places for my daily life. The long hall from the front door to the very back contained the kitchen, x-ray, rehabilitation and auditorium, as well as a hall leading to the now-familiar clinic.

The other long hall went left to the girls' ward and right to the boys' ward at the front door. Double swinging doors were at the entrance to each ward. The wards were divided into two sections. Girls, ages ten to early teens, lived on one side of the hall. Young girls and babies were on the other side. The nurses' deck was in the middle of the hall right between the two wards. The only telephone was on that desk.

I was in the older girls ward and it was divided into two sections. The main room was large enough for ten beds. The walls had fabulous paintings of fairly tale characters. One wall was all windows that were never closed because they were open to the sun porch, as we called it. This was a smaller area with eight beds all in one row against the open windows. Opposite these beds were never-opened windows that looked out over the hospital's front lawn. Each bed had a bedside table and one chair. At the end of the ward was a large playroom. In that room were books, puzzles, a record player, games and toys. The bathroom was located off the sun porch.

My first hours were spent sitting on a bed in the rather dark sun porch. I was soon to learn just how lucky I was. The sun porch was much coveted. Usually the older of these sixteen or so girls was placed out there. As in any other forced close living quarters, cliques formed. But these were always changing because every Friday someone went home or someone new arrived. So I started out with the elite of the girls' ward through no dealings of my own.

I fit right in with the girls and had no problems adjusting. In fact, I had had so much practice in switching schools that this was a breeze. And since I was on the sun porch, I had instant friends. Louise was the one girl that always stood out in my memory. She was fourteen when I first knew her, the oldest girl there. Louise had been playing dress up when she was nine years old. She and her playmate went outside to prance up and down the sidewalk in their mother's finery. It was October and neighbors were burning leaves. The edge of the Louise's trailing dress caught on fire and she ran, badly burning her legs and lower body. When I first met her, she had undergone over twenty skin graftings. Since Louise was the oldest girl on our ward, she had the bed most coveted, the last one at the end of the sun porch. This bed was slightly removed from the others to make room for traffic to the playroom. This was the only bed in the ward that had its own window.

The hospital had to run on a tight schedule with the care of so many children to consider. Everything revolved around Monday mornings. Nurses turned on the lights at six a.m. and those who could walk went to the bathroom to wash and brush teeth. Those who could not walk stayed in bed and a nurse or an aide tended to them. Breakfast came on a tray to each bed or to a table in the play room. After breakfast, we dressed and sat on our beds waiting for doctor rounds.

A group of doctors and interns came around to each bed. They talked to the child, read her chart and discussed treatment. We had to sit on our beds until every girl in our ward had been seen, then we could go to school. We left the ward as a group. Some girls were pushing others on stretchers or walking alone or wheeling themselves in a wheelchair or a cripple cart. If we got away from the nurse, we would have wheelchair races down the hall. A nurse or an aide or two accompanied us, helping when needed. We went to the two school classrooms in the hall leading to the clinic. Both boys and girls attended school together. One of these rooms was for grades three, four and five. The other room was for grades six and up. The younger children went to the auditorium for their classes. Classes changed weekly because of admissions and discharges, but we were able to keep up pretty well with our classes at home. Sometimes I would be the only child in the fourth grade and the next week there might be three of us. The classes were never very large. The teachers, one for each room, were Chicago schoolteachers.

When morning classes ended, we rushed back to the ward for lunch. But on Mondays, we were really in a hurry. By then the doctor's report would be on the nurses' desk. Some nurses let us read the doctor's report ourselves and some nurses made us ask. But, the list was always there on the desk. That list let us know who would have surgery that week, who would have a cast removed or put on, who was going to rehabilitation and who was going home. That list was our lifeline.

Doctor Sofield was the Chief Surgeon. Surgeries were only done on Tuesday and Thursday mornings. No one was afraid of going to surgery. That's what we were there for and the sooner it was accomplished, the sooner we went home. That was a given. And then, just maybe, we could pass for normal.

Mother and I had a deal. I wrote to her after the doctor's report was posted every Monday. Then she would know if I was scheduled for surgery. If I did have surgery, she could call the ward nurse that evening to see how I was doing.

Every night after supper we would watch TV. I had never seen TV before and no one I knew had a television set, so this was a really big treat. The set was on a shelf up high so all could see. Those of us on the sun porch could go into the ward to watch even if our beds had to be moved. We always were given a snack; popcorn, fruit, peanut butter bread with juice. Because of my weight problem, my treats were limited.

Bathing every day was not common in the 40's and 50's like it is today. Few people had showers in their homes. In my family, we bathed on Wednesdays and Saturdays. In the hospital we washed up every morning, but bathed and washed our hair only on Saturdays. Most girls could not get into a bathtub, so a nurse's aide washed them from a wash pan at their beds. If you were able, you went into the bathroom and took a bath in a tub. There was a large flat porcelain stand in the bathroom. It was big enough for a child to lie on. This is where we had our hair washed. We called this the "slab." After we were clean, nurses wheeled in a stretcher piled high with dresses. These dresses or usually skirts and blouses had to fit every-one, from those in a body cast to those with no cast, so fashion was not in vogue. Color and pattern was all that was important.

Friday was the day for changing sheets. From watching the nurses, we all knew how to make a bed with sharp tucked in corners. Even better than picking out the clothes you would wear for the next week, was picking out the quilt for your bed. Another stretcher was wheeled in piled with quilts made by Eastern Star ladies. The quilts were so lovely it was hard to choose. I was always looking for that special quilt I had admired the week before on someone else's bed.

Sundays were the best days of all. Parents could come for the one allowed weekly visit. They had two hours beginning at two o'clock to visit with us and only our parents could come. No brothers or sisters or other children were allowed. My parents were always there on visiting day. Our visitors could not bring us any gifts, not even gum. A nurse would patrol during visiting hours to make sure we didn't get any presents. But everyone's mother would sneak in something like hard candies or caramels. We would hide them in our glasses' cases or stationary boxes. Once we even hid candy up inside the "slab."

One day, Mother brought me a quart of fresh strawberries and I ate them when the nurse was on the other side of the ward. Then Mother took the box home and there was no evidence. On Easter Sunday, Mother brought me a gardenia corsage that I wore the two hours she was visiting. Every once in a while nurses would search our things and we would lose our stash. But next Sunday would bring more. Some girls' parents lived so far away they couldn't come every week. We all shared our goodies with them so no one was left out. All the time I spent in Chicago, my parent's came every Sunday except for one when there was heavy snow. Sometimes Mother came alone by riding on the South Shore railroad from South Bend.

Nothing happened to me for a couple of weeks. Then casts were put on both of my feet in preparation to lengthen the Achilles tendons. The doctors then changed their minds and decided the Achilles tendons' surgery could be left until later. They thought my back surgery needed to come first so the casts came off my feet. I had curvature of the spine. Today it is known as scoliosis and children are tested routinely for it without having had polio or some other disease. Special preparations needed to be made to my body before this surgery could take place.

Another girl, who was going to have the same operation, and I went down to the cast room every evening after supper and we were hung by the chin. Not as bad as it sounds, although it was not comfortable. There was a scaffold made from yellow painted iron pipes standing in the cast room. Hanging down from the top was a harness that fit over my head and under my chin. This was attached and I was hung with toes just touching the floor for five minutes. Then it was the other girl's turn. We did this for about six weeks, each night for a longer time until we could hang for thirty minutes without touching the floor

After a while this became kind of fun. The other girl would hold up comic books for me to see when I was hanging and I would do the same for her. We were never completely alone. An intern always went with us and sometimes stayed and talked to us. Sometimes he went over to the junior high classroom and played the piano. We quickly learned where he hid his cigarettes on a high shelf behind plaster cast molds. We didn't always have the same intern, but they all were fun to watch and listen to. It almost became a welcome change from our daily routine.

Christmas that year was like none I had ever had before. The Eastern Star ladies, wives of the Shriners, made or arranged for most of our gifts. One day when we came back from school, there was a huge white flocked tree in the playroom. I had never seen a flocked tree before or ever heard of such a thing. I loved to sit under it at night with just the tree lights on in the dark room. It was like magic.

Neighborhood youth groups and some student nurses came in and painted Christmas symbols on the windows. Church groups came often and sang carols. It seemed as though every day there was something special. We went down to the auditorium for parties. The presents mounted under the tree until finally we could open them. Each girl received a doll in its own suitcase filled with hand made clothes. It was just simply wonderful. There were other presents, but I only remember the doll. Mine was small only about eight inches long. Her head, arms and legs were made of something hard. But her body was soft cotton. One of her outfits was a hand knitted blue sweater with white fur around the collar.

Chapter 15

$\mathcal{A}$fter Christmas, the hangings stopped and now it was time for a cast. They put a body cast on me made of rolls of cheesecloth covered with a cold wet plaster of Paris mixture. This was extremely uncomfortable, far worse than the hangings ever were. A kind of tube stocking was put on my naked body, then the rolls of plaster were wound around and around until the cast covered me from my neck to my left hip and my right knee. It was several inches thick. My arms were free but I could not move my head.

However, the worse part was that someone had decided I would star in an educational film for medical schools. The film was to record the entire process of molding this cast on my body. I had to go to the cast room and hang while the cast was applied. While hanging I was completely undressed. I was extremely embarrassed because the room was full of strangers, all men running the cameras with big hot lights. I do not have the words to express how degraded I felt. When the process was over, I was lifted and carried to a stretcher. One of the men in charge of the filming leaned over this huge white whale and told me I did a great job and thank you. His was the only kind voice I heard that day. In today's world I think that day could have been considered child abuse. I don't know if my parents gave permission or if they were even asked or if anyone other than me ever told them. But, I never told them I was naked in front of strange men.

I requested my hospital records several years ago and I find it interesting that there is no mention of the hangings or the filming. This is what it says about preparing my spine: "... the child went through a series of wedgings and casts commencing on January 11, 1951"... the hospital records go on to detail the surgery.

I was taken back to the ward after the cast applying process was finished. This time I could not be on the sun porch. I had to be nearer the nurses' desk. Something like an electric blanket was wrapped around me to help dry the cast. But I was still very cold all night and slept little. I was now flat on my back and could not sit up. In the morning, a doctor came to check on the cast. The cast had cracked because the hot lights from the filming had made the layers of plaster dry unevenly. Back to the cast room I went and the damp cast was taken off with a small electric saw. Very scary. Then the entire procedure of putting on the cold wet body cast was repeated minus the men, cameras and lights.

The second cast dried and life went on. I learned to walk in this big heavy body case, but I could never sit down. I would walk to school pushing an empty stretcher and then lie down on it for classes. Once a week, I went back to the cast room to have holes cut in both sides of my cast at the waist. In the right side hole a block of wood was inserted as a wedge, and then rewrapped with more plaster. Each week the holes were enlarged and a larger block of wood was inserted. All this was causing me to be bend to the left, thus aligning my spine to just the proper angle. The cameramen and lights came back to film my bent over struggling walk down the long hallway. Of course, they were never pleased with the first filming and I had to repeat that walk several times, but at least I was fully dressed.

The day came when I was bent over so far I could no longer walk at all and spent my days on a stretcher or a cripple cart. A cripple cart was easier to maneuver regardless of its degrading name.

There is nothing like an itch that can not be scratched. We had all kinds of devices to reach itches within casts. A wire coat hanger was the method of choice. But in a body cast, nothing worked well. It was torture.

Now after the hangings and body casts, I was ready for surgery. This operation was called a spinal fusion. Chips of bone from my left leg were to be taken and placed in my spine in order to keep my spine in a straight position. I did not attend school the afternoon before so I could be prepped. My left leg was washed with special soap and all the hair was removed. Some kind of antibiotic ointment was put on the areas shaved and then covered with a sterile ace bandage. I was in bed so no more running around on a stretcher or in a cripple cart. Penicillin shots were started. One shot every four hours. When I was ill with the polio virus in 1946, I had so many penicillin shots, Miss Yost said my bottom looked like a pin cushion. Now they were doing it again.

Very early the next morning, Thursday, April 5, 1951, I was wheeled upstairs to the operating room. One wall was all glass. Huge lights were hanging from the ceiling. A mask was placed over my face and I could smell ether, an odor I still cannot abide. Thank goodness it is no longer used. I woke up in one of the two small private rooms behind the nurses' desk in the girls' ward late in the afternoon. I knew where I was and why. Mother knew this was the day of my operation because I had written and told her after doctor rounds on Monday. The phone on the nurses' desk rang at six o'clock. I could hear the nurse talking on the phone and then she came in and told me Mother had just called to see how I was doing. Even though I was not allowed to talk to her, that loving message from home meant so much to me.

In a day or two I was moved out of that little room and back into the general ward close to the door. I stayed in bed for about two weeks. Not going to school and having to use a bedpan was not fun. After a week or so, the black catgut stitches were removed from my leg. Each one of the forty-six stitches had to be cut and pulled out individually. My body cast had been sawed down both sides so the back half could be removed for the operation. Now the back was removed again and those stitches were removed.

When the doctors were pleased with the healing and all looked well on X-ray, the entire cast was taken off and a nurse washed my body. It felt like heaven. I had been in that cast about five months and a warm soapy wash cloth on that tender skin was blissful. Some of the dead skin was removed and all the itches rubbed not scratched because the skin was so tender. However, it didn't last long. Standing now, not hanging, they again put a body cast on me. This new cast was like freedom. It only extended from just over my shoulders and down to my hips. I could move my head and I could sit down. Also it did not take so long for it to dry.

I was back attending school in the classroom. Spring had come and I was ready to go home. After doctor rounds on a Monday in mid June, I was finally listed for dismissal for that Friday. What joy! I was going home and my baby sister had just turned one and was learning to walk. I didn't want to miss it. I wanted to be outside in the sun. And on June 22, 1951, I was.

Chapter 16

Mother, Dad and Zandra came to pick me up. My own clothes were brought to me and I struggled to get them on over my cast. I said good by and good luck to all my friends and left for home in Goshen. At home, everything looked so small. The ceiling seemed close enough to touch. I had spent eight months in a ward with a lot of open space and very high ceilings. It took me a while to adjust to a normal-sized home. Friends and relatives dropped by to welcome me home. "Normal life" at home began again, but this time I was wearing a body cast under my clothes which certainly didn't improve my silhouette.

Things at home had changed slowly from my point of view. Mother was not happy. When she was angry, she didn't talk to you and she wasn't talking to Dad. One day he came in the house and wanted to have a talk with her alone. She made me stay and listen. I did not want to hear this, but I had no choice. Apparently Dad had been unfaithful to Mother; it was not the first time. They talked and talked. I just sat there not quite believing what I was hearing and not understanding most of it. I couldn't wait for Zandra to wake up from her nap so I could go play with her and get away. Finally, some understanding was reached and family life resumed. I think these kinds of talks had gone on before. I just hadn't been involved.

Summertime was in full bloom. That meant Bible School at church, a week on the farm with my Fogel grandparents and a week at Camp Mack, our church camp on Barbee Lake. Camp was a great adventure and I loved it. We stayed in small cabins with about twelve girls in each cabin. An older girl stayed with us as a chaperone. Six old bunk beds surrounded the outside of the one room cabin and one table with four chairs was in the middle. Each bunk had its own window which was covered only with screen. If it got too cold or rained too hard, there were wooden shutters outside we could close. We hung clotheslines from bed to bed for our clothes on hangers. We kept soap, tooth brush and other grooming items in a small plastic bucket to take to the bathroom, which was a good walk from the cabins.

Early each morning during camp our activities started. First, we all gathered in a big circle for the raising of the flag and prayer. Every minute of our day was planned with classes and activities; Bible study, crafts, games, swimming with the buddy system, boating and more. The classes were mostly held in The Lodge or other buildings on the grounds. Boys had cabins on the other side of The Lodge but the boys were with us in all activities. Meals were eaten in the basement dining room in The Lodge. Six kids per table. We were assigned a table and a seat at that table. Two campers from every table took turns staying after each meal to wash and dry the dishes from their table. On Wednesday, we all went to new tables.

In the evenings we had vespers at sundown. This was held at a big campfire near the lakeshore. There were bleachers built into the hill behind the campfire. One night we would sing. Another night was communion with feet washing in the lake. And another night we had story telling. The last night of camp was always the best. We had a Pow Wow around the campfire. Mr. and Mrs. Shultz were the camp managers. Each evening over the loud speaker, Mrs.Shultz sang the Brahmans Lullaby to us after lights out. Mrs. Shultz had never cut her hair and she was probably in her fifties or sixties at that time. The night of the pow-wow she took down her usual braided bun and had two braids that reached the ground. I was amazed. Everyone dressed as Indian as possible with camp clothes and limited make up. We sang Indian type songs and listened to Indian stories.

I spent many summers at Camp Mack. They were happy times. I looked forward to getting away from home for short periods of time. I had lots of friends at camp. As I grew into my teens and still went to Camp Mack, other things became more or less important. The open-air chapel was a great place to go to think. Jacob's well was special. We had gone to Camp

Mack for special church services long before I was old enough for camp. When I was little, Dad would have to lift me up to get a cold drink from the ever-flowing water of Jacob's well.

The summer of 1952 Mother told me she was pregnant again and she cried. She didn't want to have another baby because Zandra had been such a chore and mother was thirty-seven years old. What she didn't say was now she was tied down in this ever increasingly challenging marriage. I thought another baby was a great idea, after all, I had waited many years for siblings.

Chapter 17

had to go to Chicago every three months for check ups. At one point, my body cast was removed and a plastic cast called a cellulose acetate jacket was fitted to me. It laced up in front and I could remove it for a bath once a week. Heaven! Eventually, I could take it off more and more until I stopped wearing it. I was considered obese by this time and our family doctor put me on diet pills. They made me very hyper and I had trouble getting to sleep. I was eleven.

On November 28, 1952, I was called back to Shriners Hospital for my next operation. This time I was to have surgery on both feet. Casts were put on both of my feet soon after arriving at the hospital. They were walking casts, so they didn't slow me down. Two more weeks passed and after Monday morning doctor rounds, I still was not listed on the surgery schedule. I wrote to Mother telling her I was still waiting.

On Wednesday afternoon, a nurse from our ward came to the schoolroom and took me out of class. She said a boy scheduled for surgery the next morning had the mumps and his surgery was canceled. I would have my operation in his place. She was taking me back to the ward to prep both my legs. I was glad to go to surgery, but I was extremely upset Mother didn't know. Also, since she did not know I was having surgery, she would not call to see how I was after the operation. It bothered me so much I slept very little that night. I kept praying over and over, "Please God, let my Mother know about the surgery tomorrow!"

The next morning I was the last one to go to surgery. I was put on a stretcher in the hall to wait for a surgical orderly to come get me. All the girls had to pass by me on the way to school. There I lay still worrying about my mother not knowing what was happening to me.

I had clubfeet and walked on the insides of my feet. This operation was a bilateral triple arthromeres performed on December 11, 1952. The operation was routinely used to help children with polio damage. I didn't have to stay in any special room afterwards. No medical school movies were made. The operation itself was to remove the cartilage between my ankle bones so my feet would not turn inward.

I was put back in the ward next to the door, just steps from the nurses' desk. The phone on that desk rang at six o'clock that night and I knew it was my mother. A few minutes later the nurse came to tell me that my mother had called to see how I was doing. She had not gotten my letter and wondered if I was all right. I know God had that letter misplaced because it was the only letter I ever sent Mother from the hospital in Oak Park, Illinois, that she did not receive the next day. My prayer was answered and I have never doubted it.

Everything went well. The final casts were put on my feet. They had narrow blocks of rubber in the middle on the bottom so I would not break the casts when walking on them. It was kind of like walking on short stilts. Only one problem, I couldn't walk on them and keep my balance. I needed crutches. I took classes to learn how to walk, go up and downstairs and handle other daily movements. I have always needed a banister to maneuver stairs and this was a major problem while using crutches.

My friend Louise was back in the hospital again. This was to be her last skin grafting because she was nearly sixteen. Since she was so much older, they moved her to a private room. We could go see her by going through the bathroom and the slab room into her room. If the hospital only knew what we learned in Louise's room. A rather young janitor taught us how to play strip poker. We didn't play it with him, but we knew how. He told us which nurses were sneaking down to the clinic at night to meet interns in the curtained cubicles. We thought we were learning the secrets of life and I guess we were. We discussed sex a lot. None of us knew much, but we sure did like to talk about what we thought we knew. Sometimes we were allowed to go to the little library right outside the swinging doors in the main hall. One day about five of us were in there trying to look up secret things like "penis." A doctor walked in and caught us. He was very nice and sat down and explained things and answered the questions we were willing to ask. I was just twelve and although Mother had explained the basic, I was very curious. But the idea of sex was still above my head.

Since I was mobile this stay in the hospital, I could move around the building. One of the young nurses in training asked for a couple of girls to help her. I was one chosen to help. She took us upstairs to put away Christmas decorations. We returned menus and other things to the dietitian in the kitchen. We went over to the little girls' ward and played with them. With all this touring around, I had the opportunity to look into the doctor's conference room and see the real human skeleton. Across the hall was a big glass showcase window that held the names of all the Shriners who had helped children in that hospital. George Iler's, the man who sponsored me at Shriners, name was there.

I finally completed the training for learning to walk on my new casts with crutches and was ready to go home. The doctors were in no hurry to release me, but I wanted to be home when Mom had her baby. The boys' ward was still quarantined because of mumps. But I had had the mumps years before. After I made a plea during doctor rounds, they called Mother to make sure I had had the mumps. Mother said it was true. I was dismissed on January 16, 1953.

Chapter 18

*O*n January 28, 1953 Burnell Glen Gump, my brother, was born. I was home in time. Grandma Gump came and stayed with us while Mother was in the hospital. No children were allowed to visit people in the hospital so I didn't see Burnie for several days. Zandra was two months short of being three.

Mother developed problems after Burnie's birth. First she had a tubule ligation to make sure she didn't get pregnant again. Women stayed in the hospital about a week after a normal birth. With the extra surgery she was there a few days longer. Then she developed blood clots in her right leg. For the rest of her life she took blood-thinning medications to regulate that problem.

Mother and Burnie finally came home. Now I had two siblings to help care for. Burnie was everything Zandra had not been as a baby. He slept a lot and ate on time. It was easy to care for him. Life picked up and moved on. I was now old enough to take care of both Zandra and Burnie so Mother could run to the store by herself. Zandra was more fun. I could dress her up and read to her. She didn't care if I messed up when I read stories to her from her little Golden Books.

I couldn't ride on the school bus with my stilt casts and crutches. Mom or Dad took me and picked me up each day. Dad forgot to pick me up once. I had to stand around in the school for nearly two hours after all the other kids had left. The teachers went home and there I stood in my casts with my crutches. I went outside and sat on the step. There was snow on the ground and I was cold. Mom was at home, but without a car. I never knew where Dad was, but he did finally come and get me.

Being in school wearing these stilt type casts created some problems. The boy's bathroom was right beside my classroom. But the girl's bathroom was up the stairs, across the school's entrance and down more stairs. Way too much for me to handle. Miss Patton fixed the problem by standing outside the boy's bathroom to make sure all was clear. I would then go in and use it. This was just one more degration for a handicapped child to endure. I was so glad those casts came off before the end of the school year.

Dad's chicken business was doing well. When the chickens got to be a few months old, they had to be given vaccinations in the thigh. This had to be done at night so the chickens would not panic and pile up in corners, smothering each other. Chickens at this age were no longer cute and soft. They were noisy and smelly. It took several men to help Dad and the veterinarian to vaccinate all those chickens. After all, eighteen thousand chickens have a lot of legs to be grabbed in the dark. The best way was to divide the chicken house into groups. All lights were turned off and the men would go in and grab chickens by their legs. A man could hold about three chickens in each hand. He would throw them up on a table without letting go. On this table there would be a small light and the vet would be able to see to give the shots. Then the man would take the chickens he held to a new pen and let them go. If Dad could hire enough men to help out, the job could be completed in two nights. I could watch if I stayed out of the way. It was a dirty, hot smelly job.

Dad was making a lot of money raising chickens, but it was really hard work. Since we only kept a batch of chickens about six months, we went through around thirty-six thousand chickens a year. In between each batch, the chicken houses had to be cleaned out. You can imagine the amount of chicken manure there was. It was cleaned out more often than every six months, but a really good job with soap and water and disinfectant was done only in between batches of chickens. Shoveling manure all day was backbreaking work, and the smell was terrible. So with needing a house with three bedrooms and a less physically intense job and because Dad was never satisfied with the status quo, he was making plans for a future move.

My father had also started to buy property for back taxes. He would pay the taxes on a piece of property and if the taxes weren't repaid in a certain amount of time by the former owner, Dad owned the property. He could then fix it up and sell it for a profit. Sometimes it was just a vacant lot and all that was needed to improve the property was to mow and plant a tree or two. Or it could be a house that simply needed paint before it was resold. Often Dad rented the property after the previous owners moved out. Delinquent tax properties were listed in the newspaper and Mother read these and helped with this buying of unpaid tax property venture. She would go to the tax sales and buy the properties she and Dad had thought looked promising. She really enjoyed doing that and they continued it for several years.

Waterford was a small village between Goshen and New Paris on State Road 15. At one time people forded the Elkhart River there, thus the town's name and the bridge. If you take the back way around Waterford and go along the Elkhart River on the Violet Cemetery Road, you wander through the old forest sheltering the graves. This is a lovely drive that ends at Kercher Road and another bridge. Several acres of wilderness were located at this corner and continued back to State Road 15. Tall hickory, oak, butternut and walnut trees, among others, stood over tangled brush. This land had once been a private park for the Martin family. They owned a large farm, named Martin Manor. Mr. Martin's prize-winning cattle were buried here in his park. Black squirrels were imported to live there among the nut trees. Mr. Martin was now dead and the land was left unattended.

My father bought this "park" and had it plotted into a three-street subdivision for upper middle class homes. The subdivision was named Martin Manor and the longest street was Martin Manor Drive. One of the shorter streets was named Salem Drive for the Goshen bank Dad used. With one street left to name, Dad asked me what I would like to name it. My love of all the trees influenced me to name that street Woodland Drive.

This was the beautiful area Dad had chosen for his next home and profession. The first thing to be done after all the plans were laid was to bulldoze the roads into the subdivision and I was chosen to help with that job. Dad gave me a long bamboo-fishing pole with a red rag tied at the top and showed me exactly where to stand. The driver of the bulldozer could see my flag and drive through the brush making the road straight toward me. It was hot and I was sweating. Flies and other critters kept flying in my face and hair and sometimes they bit. I didn't realize I was helping to make history; I was just plain ready to go home.

Chapter 19

$\mathcal{W}$hile Dad went headfirst into his new adventure, Mom and I took care of Zandra and Burnie. I dressed Zandra up in pretty dresses and played games with her. Burnie was still such a good baby that Mother started to relax. We also prepared to move, again.

The summer passed. I went to camp and to visit Grandma Fogel and my cousins. Grandma still made me take a nap every afternoon. She would not let me go out in the barnyard alone. She was afraid a man would be hiding in the barn. She had more fears than most people. Life was getting harder for her.

While at Grandma Fogel's I had found some old books in a trunk in the attic. She reluctantly let me take them. She had never read them. They had belonged to one of her brothers. The books were English romance novels where ladies wore chiffon frocks not dresses. I started to read them while sitting alone on the attic floor. I enjoyed reading them. There was no one to make fun of me when I mispronounced a word.

Back home Mother continued preserving fruits as they came into seasons. Freezing was becoming more popular. We now had an automatic washer and dryer in the basement. We often went to Syracuse Lake in the late afternoons for a swim and picnic at the public beach. I took swimming lessons a couple of times, but never learned to swim. Aunt Melba and her kids came with us once and she brought a pizza pie! It was like a deep-dish casserole.

While we were busy canning peaches, drying corn, freezing green beans and caring for Zandra and Burnie, Dad was building his first house in Martin Manor. It was a light blond-colored brick house with three bedrooms and a full basement. The garage sat back from the house just a bit.

The house was ready for us to move into before school began that fall of 1953. I started seventh grade at Waterford Elementary School. With my casts and crutches gone since the early spring, I was able to walk to school across a field until I reached Road 15 and then I walked along the road to school. During bad weather, Mother took me and picked me up.

Burnie had started crawling and walking around the furniture that fall. Soon after Christmas I started trying to teach him to walk. After a week or so, he took his first steps alone. He was walking by his first birthday, which seemed to be a big accomplishment. However, it backfired on me. Now he could turn the knobs on the TV and completely mess up my life.

Shriner's Hospital was ready for my final operation. I was admitted on April 30, 1954. I was thirteen and Zandra had just turned four. Burnie was nearly one and a half. It was harder to leave home this time. But I wasn't gone for long. I was there this time to correct drop foot in my right foot only. They planned to transfer a tendon from the back of my weak right leg to the front of my foot so I could lift that foot when I walked. All went as planned and the surgery was performed on May 13, 1954.

School was still in session since Chicago had school until June 22 that year. But with the warmer longer days, we could go outside for a while after classes and on Saturdays. A door in the playroom, normally never unlocked, was opened. It led down a ramp bordered by honeysuckle bushes into a fenced grassy yard. We could spend some time out there and it was a treat to be in grass and sunshine. We could see normal kids in the neighborhood walking home from school. Sometimes they stopped at the fence and talked to us. They were never nasty, just curious, asking us questions about why we had a cast on or did we like to ride in a wheelchair? I'm sure we looked strange to them in all our different kinds of mobility contraptions.

The outside door in the playroom had a mate just opposite in the sun porch. It also had a ramp but no one ever went out that door. During warm weather that door was left open during the day. On Sunday visiting days, Mother and Dad brought Zandra and Dad would walk her up that ramp to see and talk to me through the screen. It was probably against the rules, but meant a lot to me.

One Saturday we had a special treat. All the older girls went down to the boys' ward and out through their playroom door down their ramp and into their orchard! The hospital had a picnic set up for us including hot dogs with all the fixings. Hard to believe how such a small thing made our day seem extra special.

I went home on June 23, 1954. We went back to Chicago in one month to have the cast removed. After that I went back for check ups and x-rays until I was permanently discharged on September 2, 1955, less than a month before my fifteenth birthday.

The Shriner's Children Hospital completely changed my life for the better. I was still handicapped, but my body was straighter and I walked with a less prominent limp. I could wear normal clothes and shoes and blend into a crowd. The hangings by the chin and filming occasions are now just a memory, along with many other joyful and sad times. All in all, I was content during my hospital stays because I belonged and didn't have to prove to anyone that I was just as good as they were. Children from every cultural background were patients with me and we were all alike no matter what our disabilities were. I learned there is always someone with more problems than mine. As long as I live there will be people staring and pointing at my differences. But my life has been abundantly fuller because of Shriner's Hospital and I am a better person because of it.

Chapter 20

$\mathcal{D}$ad built houses and sold land. Martin Manor began to look like a subdivision with all the new people moving in. We moved again in the fall of 1954, but we didn't go far. Dad built an Indiana limestone house at the corner of Martin Manor Drive and Violet Road. The living room was long with a picture window facing west and overlooked the bend in the Elkhart River. Dad had an office in this house. The walls of his office were decorated in pecky cypress wood, which at the time was considered "classy."

This house was so close to the river that the yard was used by turtles as a nursery for their eggs. Mother turtles dug holes, laid their eggs and returned to the water. I would stand right beside them and watch. Later when the eggs hatched, we had baby turtles by the dozens all over our yard.

I started eighth grade at Waterford Elementary School. I was only here for a few months because we moved to Sebring, Florida. We had been going to Florida during Christmas break for the past few years. Dad looked for that right place to build houses for the winter. Mother enrolled me at Sebring Junior High, which was in the same building with the high school. What a shock! I was one of the smartest kids in my class and never had homework. A few kids came to school barefooted. The atmosphere of the school was impoverished and less academic than in Goshen. This was entirely new to me, but again I tried to fit in and I knew to be unseen would help prevent problems for me.

Dad bought two lots in the middle of a small orange grove near a big golf resort hotel and started building two houses. We rented a furnished house across the street from the church. I walked about four blocks to school every day and Zandra started nursery school around the corner. We settled in and started over.

The church, as usual, became the focal point of our lives. This was a big church. The youth had an active group that I was encouraged to join. Karen became my best friend. There was a boy named James who was "tall, dark and handsome." Best of all, he was nice to me. I turned fourteen that September. I had never discussed dating with Mother. But then there was James. In the high school band and sixteen, James had an old Plymouth car that he and his older brother, David, built.

At every church service, the entire youth group of about ten to fifteen kids sat together in the church balcony. It was like we had our own club in church. Church often led to a bunch of us riding around in the car with James afterward. We usually took Karen home because she lived out in the country. We'd drive down a sandy road between rows of orange trees. And then there was a clearing to Karen's house. Her family did not have much money. Most of the kids slept on mattresses on the floor. The toilet was outside. In Southern traditional, Karen had to say "Yes, Sir" or "No, Mame" when she spoke to her parents.

The town of Sebring was segregated in the 1950's, like most Southern cities. A siren sounded at ten o'clock every night and all black people had to be in their side of town. The only excuse to be out was to have a work permit. One evening James drove through the black section of town after ten o'clock. The main street was not paved and there were very few streetlights. But the sides of the street were full of people visiting back and forth. It was not scary as imagined. People were talking, laughing and even singing. The neighborhood was much friendlier than the white part of town.

Often we pooled our money and bought gas for James. Thirty cents was enough gas for an evening of riding around. Six or seven of us were always in the car. I belonged for the first time and I felt accepted.

One week there was a movie showing at the theater downtown. The movie starred Doris Day and Rock Hudson. Mother said I could walk over and see it after school. I did, all by myself. On my way home, James passed by in his car. He stopped and gave me a ride home. The next time our group of friends went out for a ride, he asked me to sit in front in the middle. During the evening he took my hand. I nearly died from the shock as electricity shot through my body. We had a real date soon after that. Karen and her boyfriend went with us. James took me home last and walked me to the door and kissed me. My first kiss. I don't know how I got in the house. I tried to be very quiet, as I thought everyone was asleep, I did not turn on the lights.

In my own room I found my bed was full of stuff. All the rolls of toilet tissue in the house, kid's toys, books, shoes and oranges were piled high in my bed. Dad thought it was a great joke. I didn't think it was very funny. Apparently my parents watched the entire kiss through the window.

James and I dated a few more times. We sat together in the balcony at church. I believe I was the "good-girl-novelty" to him. James was kind to me and did more wonders for my lagging self-esteem than he ever knew.

Near the first of February, Dad's houses were built and sold. It was time to move back to Indiana. Of course, I did not want to leave my friends. Karen and I kept in touch until I went to college. We went back to Sebring for short two-week vacations several more times over my teen years. I saw James again. When he was eighteen, he was in the back seat of a car with several band members on his way to a football game. A train hit their car. James was the only one killed.

We moved back into our limestone house and I was back in Waterford School to finish the eighth grade. No more easy school work and fooling around. I worked for my grades. My best friends were Patty and Pat. Every day we walked home from school together.

At the end of the year, the PTA held a big school party. The kids in every grade sang songs or read poetry. Then the parents had a cakewalk.

I never went to a cakewalk, but cakewalks were very popular fundraisers at that time. Mothers baked cakes and brought them to school that night. As I was talking with some friends, a boy came running down the stairs and into the room. My dad had just bought a cake for five hundred dollars. I knew there would be trouble at home that night. But nothing much was said. Mother froze the cake and said at that price we would make it last for years. Apparently Dad didn't want someone outbidding him for this plain ordinary cake. I never had any idea who made it, but Dad had made up his mind the other guy was not going to have it. I don't ever remember eating that cake.

Dad did more irrational things. He yelled at us for using too much toilet paper, or not turning out lights or leaving the refrigerator door open too long. It got to the point that I had a sick feeling when I heard him open the door to come into the house. From the very beginning after moving into this house on the bank of the river, I escaped this family tension by going to the Violet cemetery. It was a nice place to walk. After a big funeral, I would take a few flowers from that new grave and put them on a grave that never received any flowers. There was a grave for a baby who died on my birthday and I always put flowers on that grave. This large cemetery had old large trees and the Elkhart River flowing around the edge. It was like a park. The keepers of the cemetery got to know me and saved the prettiest ribbons for me when they took the dead bouquets off graves.

Our house was close to the river and the bridge over the Elkhart River that overlooked a popular fishing spot. Violet Road ran between our house and the high riverbank. Men would often fish near the bridge. The bank was so high it had guardrails and they would have to get down to the water using a path near the bridge, and then they could walk a little bit until there was a path up the high bank to the road. I liked to go to the bridge and stand there and watch the water and throw stones. One day on my way home from the bridge for lunch, a fisherman came up the path and started talking to me. He wanted me to go down and fish with him, but I knew I would be in trouble if I didn't get home in time for lunch. He told me to come back after lunch. I mentioned this at home when we were eating lunch. Dad immediately stood up and left the house. I was told never to talk to the fishermen and never to go to the bridge alone.

The summer of 1955 I kept myself busy. I spent a week helping out at Bible school and a week at Camp Mack. But most of my summer I spent with my friends Pat and Patty. Pat lived right on the river and she had a rowboat. We three would take off and row up and down the river and explore tributaries and anything that looked interesting. We found abandoned shacks and small caves. We knew where the water lilies grew and where to find the biggest turtles and frogs. None of us swam well, but we didn't think about things like drowning. Mother knew I went row boating on the river, but had no idea how far we went or how dangerous it could have been.

With summer almost over I started having a lot of anxiety about high school. I was fearful of going up and down stairs carrying books with people trying to push me out of the way. Trying to get books out of my locker, walking to class on time and going up steps all seemed like a nightmare to me. I didn't tell anyone, but I thought about it all the time. I was very self-conscious. Still "crippled," fat, with a crooked smile, still afraid to read out loud and make a fool of myself. Regardless of my fears, the day came to start school at Goshen High.

Chapter 21

$\mathcal{My}$ freshman year at Goshen High School was not great. I would get ready long before bus time in the morning and I often needed to go in the bathroom to throw up. Now I understand I was having anxiety attacks. I was afraid I would miss the bus, or lose a book or the very worse thing of all, fall down or be the cause of students slowing down while they waited behind me to climb the stairs. Every morning I went through this anxiety and never told Mother or anyone.

I worked in the truancy office during study hall time. I went to every classroom on all three floors to collect attendance slips that were hung outside each door after every period. I collected them after lunch. I made lists of kids who were absent. Working in that office was good for me. I was able to navigate the building well without crowds around and began to feel more comfortable. After several months, my anxiety began to decrease.

I finally got another dog. This time we went to a breeder. I picked out a blond Pomeranian female puppy and called her Ching. Dad would not let her stay in the house. He made her stay in the garage at night. Pomeranians are housedogs, and before long it was obvious I could not keep her. At least she was sold, and not shot.

That summer between my freshman and sophomore years, my friends and I sat around dreaming of guys. We went to parties and picnics, but always in groups. Every time I left the house Mother reminded me it only took "one evening to ruin the rest of my life." I heard that for years. I never even came close.

Patty started dating Philip; a college-aged guy that lived in Waterford. Philip had a friend, Johnny. Johnny was 21. His dad was the music director of the little church in Waterford. Johnny was a really nice guy. A bunch of us would go riding around in Johnny's car. He worked at a gas station and as far as I know he always did. He would come and sit and watch TV with me when I was babysat Zandra and Burnie. Philip and Johnny went on a trip that summer and Johnny sent me a card from Salt Lake City with a little bag of salt sewn on the side. It made my summer a little more exciting.

New Paris had had a dairy for as long as I could remember. It was called the New Paris Creamery. Suddenly, it became Burgers Dairy and began doing very well. Mr. Burger wanted to buy our house *so we moved again.* Dad had built two new houses on Woodland Drive and we moved into one of them while he had Mother's "dream house" built. With Goshen College in town, Dad put up a bulletin board notice asking for help and we had plenty of young men to move our belongings two blocks.

I turned sixteen that September of 1956. Mother was determined to give me a sweet sixteen-birthday party. She arranged a date for me for the football game that Friday night. It was a surprise! When I answered the door, it was Johnny. I hadn't seen him for several months. After the game, Mom had set up a scavenger hunt for six couples of my friends. And after that was food with birthday cake and ice cream. At midnight the boys had to go home. The girls and I had a slumber party in the empty house next door that Dad had built and not yet sold. It was a great party.

Johnny gave me a designer tube of lipstick. I kept it until I went to college. I never had another date with Johnny or with anyone else while in high school. Once when I came home from college with a car full of my girl friends, I stopped for gas at the station where Johnny worked and he put gas in my car. He was married.

During my sophomore year of high school, we were assigned in literature class to read a book of our choice and to give an oral book report not exceeding ten minutes. We were given several weeks to prepare. I still had some books from Grandma Fogel's attic, which included the paper back movie edition of *Gone with the Wind*. I thought that I could look at the pictures and make up a report without reading the book. I had not seen the movie. But I started reading the book and was hooked. I read every word, all 1135 pages and loved every minute. Most of the other kids read books like *Big Red Finds a Home* or *Betty's Prom Dress*.

I got up to give my ten-minute book report and was so enthused I forgot to be afraid. When I sat down, the room was quiet. The teacher said it was obvious I enjoyed reading the book. My oral report took twenty minutes and he didn't stop me. That was the turning point in my problems with reading. Even though I did not read a book again unless it was assigned, I learned three very valuable things. One, reading can be fun, especially if you are lonely; two, a book can be a great friend. Third, I learned not to be afraid of standing up in front of people when what I was talking about was important and interesting.

We moved into Mother's dream home later that year. The perfect house was made of Mother's first and only choice, Indiana limestone. The house was one story and built on the corner of Martin Manor and Salem Drives. Being on a corner lot was special. Floor to ceiling windows faced both streets and facing southeast the rooms were always filled with sunshine. The kitchen was on the side of the house facing Salem Drive. Mother had planned her favorite room carefully with a window over the sink and a large window in the eating area. She had more cupboards than even she could completely fill. There was a desk just for her and places for her house plants. She always said doing the dishes together was the best time to talk to her children but now she had a dishwasher and a garbage disposal. The dishwasher was used only when we had guests. There were several tall old trees in the yard, which meant lots of leaf raking in the fall. But we all loved trees. Burnie had the unsettling habit of being at the top of a tree when Mother called for supper.

There were three large bedrooms along the west side of the house.

My room was the front corner room. Matching drapes and bedspreads were made for my new twin beds. Every bedroom had large closets and built in drawers and cupboards. Mother and Dad's room had its own bathroom. I shared the family bathroom with my siblings.

This perfect house was truly lovely. Even the two-car garage behind the kitchen wing was finished in knotty pine wood. The utility room was bigger than some bedrooms we had in other houses. Mother had every new idea in home styling she knew of put into her perfect house.

Outside, Mother finally had her tea rose garden. I had to dust the roses for aphids early in the morning and after every rain shower. I disliked roses after doing that day after day. Not only did Mother have her rose garden, she had room for flowers all along the back fence. She planted things she hadn't planted before like Canterbury bells, gladiolas, and her sister Melba's favorite iris. At the very end of the front entrance sidewalk, Dad had put enough gravel in for a small parking area. From this parking area the front walk led to the house and low shrubbery was planted on either side of the walk near the street. In between these bushes, Mom planted many shockingly pink petunias. It was one of my jobs to deadhead these petunias after their first flowers began to fade. This encouraged the plant to bloom even more and get bushier. These pink petunias became famous in the neighborhood. Everyone commented on how beautiful they were. Mother planted them every spring.

This was the house that was perfect and so the family would now be perfect in every way. It was a nice house and a nice dream. And that was all it was.

Junior year of high school started. That year I was in the school choir, which was a pleasure and a problem for me. The choir director allowed me to stand on the floor instead of struggling upon the risers when the choir sang before an audience. When the choir went away to perform in contests, they were required to enter an auditorium and parade down the aisles and up the steps onto the stage. Steps without railings I could not handle, so I would play sick and stay home.

My new best friend was Joy. She was attractive and intelligent but she was quiet and kept to herself. Joy couldn't wait to grow up and get out of Goshen. She was from a Mennonite family and she wanted to live free of their hold on her. We had sleepovers and made pizza from a box mix made by Chef Boyardee. Joy was very creative. She painted her small bedroom in stripes and solid colors of lavender, light green and white. I was amazed how beautiful it was.

Dad taught me to drive in our big green Roadmaster Buick. That fall we went to Huntertown for a visit and I was allowed to drive home. Dad was very critical, but I did it without mishap. After that, Mom let me drive now and then down to the grocery store. There were no super markets but there were neighborhood stores in town and a small store down the road. Since learning to drive, it was not cool to ride the bus to school and I never did again. Joy could get her mother's car and she would pick me up and take me to school.

Being able to drive meant I could take my little sister to the movies. I took her and it was a disaster for me. I don't remember what movie we saw but some neat high school boys sat in front of us. I tried hard to be suave. Zandra was all dressed up with her Mary Jane shoes. During the movie one shoe came off and fell down the step under the seat in front of us. I had to get the usher and his flashlight to find it for us. I was so embarrassed. Unfortunately, that day was just the beginning of movie mishaps with my sister.

At Christmas, I wanted to have a special tree in our large living room windows. My idea was to have a white flocked tree (like in Shriner's Hospital) with clusters of three bright pink balls placed on the tree without traditional tree lights. In place of lights, I wanted two spotlights shining up under the tree. Mother liked the idea and we set about getting it done. Dad had a fit. We did it anyway and it stood in the living room. It wasn't long before the president of the bank complimented Dad on his beautiful Christmas tree. Soon other business people and neighbors were talking about it. An electric company asked to photograph it for ads in other states. My idea was a hit. One year mother made Zandra, Burnie and me sit in front of the tree in our pajamas and have a picture taken for Christmas cards.

Zandra may have started life screaming but she was a delightful child. I loved dressing her up in pretty frilly dresses that I could never wear. Her hair was long, blond and very curly. When she went to birthday parties, I put her hair on top of her head with a yellow rose bud in it. I was living out my fantasies through her.

When Burnie started school, Mother noticed he couldn't hear well. She took him to the doctor. The doctor found that when Burnie had stuck an eraser end of a pencil in his ear, the eraser had broken off. He had surgery to replace some parts of his inner ear.

Mother had gone back to teaching at Waterford Elementary School. All of us were in school now and she needed her career. However, she only had a two-year normal degree and by the 1950's she needed a bachelor's degree to keep her life teacher's license. She started taking a class or two at Goshen College. Dad made money but became more mentally unstable, although we didn't see it at the time.

Chapter 22

$\mathcal{My}$ third year of high school ended. Mother took courses at the college all through summer. She paid me to clean the house weekly. During my cleaning, I found a pack of cigarettes between the stack of clean sheets in her bedroom cupboard. Seemed there were secrets all around.

Mother made friends with a fellow teacher who supplemented her teaching income by making and selling ceramics. At one point she bought a new kiln, and Mother bought her old one for me. So I started making ceramic jewelry. I sold the jewelry at a hat shop downtown in Goshen. I never made a lot of money, but it was fun. I did make and sell four ceramic Christmas trees and made enough money to buy a good winter coat and my high school class ring. Dad flat out refused to buy the ring for me. When working with ceramics, my biggest problem was Mother. I would get going on a project, have everything laid out in order and then I would have to go to bed. Next day, Mother would have put it all away. Cleaning up every night became a running battle between us.

By the end of June, things got bad between father and me. I know we had a big fight, but apparently I blocked most of it from my memory. My brother Burnie remembers the fight. He was still very young and it was the first time he saw Dad lose control. Burnie told me I had brought home a puppy and was in the process of putting down newspapers and fencing off a part of the utility room for him when Dad came home. Burnie heard yelling and came running and saw Dad hitting me. I do remember being sent down to a vacant lot to hoe our garden. But I have no memory of the dog, so guess it was gone when I came home from hoeing.

The next day, Mother took me to Aunt Melba's big house in Flushing, Michigan. I stayed there nearly a month. Aunt Melba had always gone out of her way to be especially kind to me with gifts and attention.

Staying with her was just an extension of that. She took me to Merle Norman and got me a complete facial and lessons on how to apply make up. She bought the entire make up kit for me. She showed me her ceramic kiln and work shop in the basement. She made large formal dinners for the family in the evenings at home. We sat at her enormous dining room table.

Aunt Melba had a black maid come in daily. She did all the general housework. When she was doing the laundry, she set up the ironing board in the spare bedroom upstairs at the head of the back staircase. That way she could run down quick if needed. I liked to just sit in there and visit with her. I don't remember anything we ever talked about and I don't remember her name.

One day I got a sand flea bite on the surgery incisions on my right leg. The bite became infected and Uncle Andy had to give me a shot of penicillin. His doctor's office was in a back wing of the house so I went back there with him and he gave me an injection. Before I left to go home, he gave me another one because the bite was still not healed.

As soon as I was home and unpacked, I started packing again to go with the church youth group to North Carolina. I think Mom had this all planned so I was away from Dad as long as possible. The youth members had raised enough money to pay for several of us to go on a chartered bus to Lake Lejeune in North Carolina. I'm sure most of my friends remember many different things about that trip. I don't remember much. I do remember the girls from Goshen stayed in a motel with girls from other states. The conference itself was in a gated compound with a large auditorium. The entire place was overrun with teenagers from every state from the Church of the Brethren.

In the auditorium we all met daily for singing and prayer services. The singing was magnificent. That many kids belting out songs we all knew since early childhood was very moving and thundering. I did miss one of the big assemblies because the place on my leg where the sand flea had bitten me was very swollen again. I went to the first aid station and they had me lay on a cot to await the doctor. While lying there I could hear to all those other kids singing their hearts out without me. The doctor put a new dressing on the bite and sent me on my way. Leaving the compound that night, every car was stopped at the gate and asked if we knew a girl with a hurt leg. They never found her. Later, I discovered it was me that they were looking for to recheck my fleabite.

Upon returning home I found another problem waiting for me. Aunt Melba's maid had received a post card from Roxann and Aunt Melba was upset because I didn't send her one. In truth, I didn't have time to send anyone a post card, not even my own mother. Aunt Melba never talked to me about this. The news all came through Grandma Fogel. From then on, I was pretty much ignored by Aunt Melba and nothing was ever said directly to me about it. Months later Grandma told mother the maid discovered the lady sitting beside her in choir at her church was named Roxanne, before she had only ever known her by her last name. It was that Roxanne who had sent the post card.

Back home things were under control on the surface. It was just an unspoken truth that Dad was running around on Mom. We all knew it. Zandra and Burnie were probably too young to understand, but I did. Things were just not right and Mother was not happy, but away from home no one knew how miserable she was. Finally there was a show down and Mother faced Dad with facts he could not deny. I was asked to sit in on this, the last place on earth I wanted to be. I felt like I was outside looking through a window onto someone else's life. We three sat in the family room of the perfect house and they talked it out. There was crying and wringing of hands on both sides. Dad promised it would never happen again. They took out their wedding vows and read them to each other. We got down on our knees and prayed for God's help. It was all very draining, but hopeful. We began having more family prayer time and holding hands during meal prayers. Both of my parents tried to make this family work. But doubt was always present. Dad didn't have, nor want, the kind of job where Mother would always know where he was and could reach him. I always felt like I was walking on eggs.

Color photographs of good quality were still uncommon. So Dad had given our neighbor, Evelyn Frick several 4x6 black and white pictures of all the houses he had built and she used special photo paints and colored them. They were mounted, famed and hung on the family room fireplace. After the heart-wrenching family meeting, my parents gave Evelyn their hand written wedding vows and she wrote them in calligraphy on parchment paper. Mother had them framed and hung above the fireplace as a reminder the marriage was starting over.

In the fifties, I knew no one who was divorced, except the crazy lady who lived next to Evelyn. And she was from Chicago, so what did you expect? Patty's parents were divorced, but she had such a great stepfather we never thought about her real father. Divorce just wasn't an option for Mother. I believe she truly thought Dad could change and that he was worth sticking it out with. Probably more than anything, she was afraid of what people would think and say, especially Grandma Gump.

My senior year of high school started with all these family issues in the background. I was now president of the somewhat academically elite club The Scribblers, although I was never on the honor roll. I was in Miss Zook's Senior English Literature class and even enjoyed Beowulf. Senior year was good.

Joy and I still drove to school. It was tradition in Goshen before the Homecoming football games in the fall to have a snake dance from the school to downtown. Everyone would leave the building before the last bell holding hands and "snake" through town. I never could physically do that, but it looked like fun. I never went to a dance or a prom. I never had a date after my sixteenth birthday party. But I did have red suede shoes.

After a ball game in Elkhart, Joy, some other girls and I went window-hopping and saw some great red suede shoes. Joy bought a pair and I went back when I could get the car and bought a pair for myself. That was the first time I wore hose to school. Hose were so grown up but also such a pain with garter belts and seams down the back.

Two important events happened that year, 1958-59. Grandpa and Grandma Fogel left the farm and moved into a small house in Huntertown next to their church. Grandpa had an old Buick he parked behind the house and he would sit in it for hours at a time. He didn't have a barn any more where he could go to get away from Grandma, so he sat in his car. He didn't read or anything, just sat there. In the summer he had a big garden to work in. Or he sat in a lawn chair and watched the garden grow. My dad built a closed-in porch onto this house for them. Grandma had her washer and dryer out there and a freezer.

Grandma Gump died in February 1959. She died in her sleep, just as peacefully and quietly as she had lived her life. But it was a shock to all because she had not been ill. She was 75. Her funeral was in New Paris, but the family brought her body back to the old church cemetery along the Eel River near Churubusco. My aunts made up a box of Grandma's every-day belongings and gave them to the grandchildren. I was given one of her aprons, her rolling pin and her thimble among other things. Real treasures to me.

No one took Grandma's death harder than my father did. He loved and admired his mother a great deal. And with her death, he seemed to lose just a bigger piece of his sanity. About two years before she died, Dad built his parents a new house in New Paris. It was the normal three-bedroom ranch, but it had a nice screened-in porch on the back where she sat and did her hand sewing or shelled peas. I was the first guest they had for dinner in that house. When I started high school, Grandma told me to enjoy it because it would be the fastest four years of my life. She was right.

I wanted to go far away to college in another state. It sounded so adventurous. I wanted to be a writer. Well, Mother had other ideas. I would go to Manchester College and I would study teaching so I could support myself. That spring, Mother and I visited Manchester College and were given the grand tour. I was enrolled in the elementary education department. I didn't have a lot to say about it, but it was okay with me. I think I would have agreed to anything in order to leave home.

I still had to graduate. In the spring before the end of school, I was home alone for lunch one day and the phone rang. It was a woman asking for Herbert, my dad. When I said he was not there and could I take a message, she would not give me her name and started asking me questions such as who was I and how old was I. I knew this was big trouble. It took me a day or two, but I did tell Mother. After that phone call the wedding vows over the fireplace disappeared and I never saw them again.

Dad's temper became shorter and not just with us. I never heard him swear. But he would roll down his car window and scream out at someone he thought had taken his parking place at church. Things got scary again. And then it was time for me to graduate from high school. Dad didn't think he could make it because he had a "business meeting" in Elkhart that evening, which I didn't believe. I was so worried about walking across the stage and getting up and down the steps without falling, I didn't know if he was there or not. Later I found out he was there with Mother and my sister and brother. Mother gave me a pearl ring. Mother and Dad also gave me luggage. After graduation, I went out with my friends to several open houses other parents were having for their graduating children.

That summer I baby-sat neighbor's kids. I still cleaned for Mom while she took classes. I still took care of Zandra and Burnie and I packed. I couldn't wait to get out of that perfect house. One day Mother asked me to go to Burger's Dairy in New Paris to buy milk. For some unknown reason they were giving away boxes of chocolate covered cherry flips. I got a box and hid the candy in a drawer under my pajamas. Over a week, I ate all those luscious nuggets by myself. That was my form of intoxication.

Chapter 23

eptember 1959 couldn't come quickly enough. Freshmen had to be on campus a few days early for orientation. I lived in Oakwood Hall, the larger and by far the older of the two dorms for girls. Every freshman lived in a dorm and was not allowed to have a car the first semester. Oakwood Hall was a large red, brick three-story building. The cafeteria was in the basement and there was an attic for storage. All the floors and stairs were made from wood making them creaky and spooky late at night. A porch covered the entire front of this building. My friends and I spent many hours sitting on that porch talking about the world and our personal problems.

From the very beginning, I had friends. Several of us who lived in the same hall started to hang around together. Linda, Peggy, Jean and I became friends. Peggy's brother, Bill was also at Manchester. Bill had several guy friends that were part of this group of kids that I hung out with. From my dorm room we could see if Bill had parked his old convertible car on the street. Once we filled his car with balloons. Then we sat in my room and waited for him to find it. We thought it was hilarious even if he didn't think it was so funny.

College became a place where I felt safe and I was having a great time. Classes became a sideline to my college career. But after grades came out, I got the message loud and clear from home to settle down and study. So I studied enough to pass my classes. I learned other things too. Like how to play Rook, and just hang out. I wasn't used to having so much free time. I only went to classes four hours each day and chapel twice a week. The rest of the time I had to do something besides studying. Classes were mostly boring.

It soon became clear that I was happy at college and I wasn't in a big hurry to go home on weekends. Because it was difficult to find a ride home, Dad bought me a 1953 Pontiac for three hundred dollars with the understanding I would pay him back. Now I was in "hog heaven." On Saturday nights, kids would pile into my car and we would drive downtown to a movie in North Manchester. I think we saw every movie that came to town. I was even able to get the theater to change the starting time for "South Pacific." I had to guarantee I could get fifty girls there for the management to change the time. Otherwise, the movie ran longer than our ten o'clock curfew. I did it. I loaded the car up, making several trips and had the girls there. We had no seat belts in those days so we could pile them in.

Smoking and dancing were not allowed on campus. So if I parked my car across the street, friends who smoked could sit in my car. We had our own little clubhouse going on. I did not smoke, but I sat there and listened to all the talk and felt like I belonged.

Freshmen ate in the dining room at assigned seats during the week. So we could only eat out on weekends. But often we went down to a small restaurant behind the college called The Coachhouse to get out of the dorm and have a coke. Sometimes Bill took us down there in his car. One night during that first winter I went to the Coachhouse with some friends, but Bill took me back to the dorm. It was cold and snowing. He stopped in the middle of the road and looked at me. I was just a little scared. He said, "Do you want to do something you have never done before?" I wasn't sure what he had in mind until he started to put the top down on his convertible. We rode all around the campus in the snow with the top down.

Mother liked to hear all about what I was doing in college with my friends. She loved the story of Bill taking me for a ride in his convertible with his car top down. I soon learned to tell Mom only what I wanted the world to know. She would get on the phone and call everyone she knew and tell them what I had said. Sometimes I confided in her and was very disappointed when she disregarded my feelings and told other people. I now realize she was living through me because her marriage was such a disappointment.

I went home for Christmas only to find things were no better. Everything looked happy and pleasant but there was an undercurrent. For one thing, Dad bought really nice expensive gifts for Mother and me. He gave each of us a Pendleton wool blazer. Mine was blue and burgundy and forty plus years later, I still wear it. Dad also gave Mom a mink hat. I had never known him to go out and shop for anyone before. That could only mean something was wrong. The entire vacation lasted way too long. I couldn't wait to get back to my new friends.

When school was out for the summer, I went home and found my friends from high school had moved on with their lives. I didn't see them. I had not seen Pat and Patty for a long time. Pat married her high school boyfriend and never finished high school. She died young. I don't know what happened to Patty.

Dad had started to build some houses for wealthy people from Chicago. He thought he had gone as far as he could go in Goshen and he started talking about moving to Fort Wayne. A family came along and made an offer on "the perfect house" and Dad sold it. I have no idea what Mother's input was in any of this. But I knew she loved that house and hated leaving all her friends in Goshen. However, the perfect house had not brought her happiness.

Dad went to Fort Wayne and picked out a house on Ravenswood Drive just north of Fort Wayne. He bought it from a German professor who was returning to Germany with his family. The professor and his family had brought their furniture with them from Germany and didn't want the cost of shipping it back home. So Dad bought their furniture too. The rest of the summer was spent packing as fast as possible. Dad would never hire a moving van, but he rounded up relatives and friends and took two days to move everything from Goshen to Ravenswood Drive in Fort Wayne. They were the hottest two days of that year, over one hundred degrees both days. Almost everything we owned was stored in the two-car garage because the house was full of furniture already. The house was fine but nothing like the house we left. Because I was away at school most of the time, it was really not so important to me.

After I helped with the move, I went back to college. Jean and I were roommates that year. We lived in the newer girls' dorm, East Hall. We became friends with a new girl, Gail, who lived across the hall from us. Gail had transferred from Northwestern to be closer to her boyfriend. Gail and I were both in elementary education and Jean was studying social studies. Gail was an excellent student. She helped motivate us into getting serious about college. Things came easily to Jean. She would wait until the night before an exam, then stay up all night to study and do fine. I had to struggle along and I could never put assignments off.

One of the highlights of my sophomore year was my trip with Gail to Northwestern University in Evanston, Illinois. She had told us how unfriendly that school was and how wealthy most of the girls were. Some didn't see their parents from year to year. They just called home and asked for money and went to Europe or wherever for the summer. It was hard for me to visualize that kind of life. Northwestern had dorms that filled up fast. Then the university rented entire floors in near by hotels for the overflow of girls to stay in. These girls had phones in their rooms and came and went as they pleased. What a surprise this was to me. Gail had gone to Northwestern her freshman year, but she disliked large campus life and found the friendly smallness of Manchester much more appealing.

While in Chicago we took the El downtown and did some shopping. We also went to see "The Miracle Maker." We sat in the lobby of the Palmer House Hotel and watched the people, trying to guess who was meeting their husband, wife or lover. I was amazed at how many people just sat around doing nothing. Two friends of Gail's from Northwestern met us there and we went out for dinner. We walked to The Town and Country restaurant. They had escargot on the menu and no paper towels in the restroom. You had to give a lady twenty-five cents to use a towel that she handed you. This was a completely new world to me.

I went home the weekend I turned twenty-one. Mother, Dad, and another couple took me out for dinner at the Carousel on Coliseum Boulevard in Fort Wayne. It was a very nice bar and restaurant. I had my first alcoholic beverage, an Old Fashion. I thought anything with cherries in it would taste good. Wrong. I also wore my first and only pair of high heels. They were lovely brown shoes with fabric bows on the toes. I could not stand still in them because it was like walking on stilts. Also, the shoes really hurt my feet and legs. I had trouble enough walking in my flat shoes.

Dad had bought a small house for back taxes a few years before. The house was in Hobart, Indiana and he rented it for thirty-five dollars a month. He gave me that money as my monthly spending money in college. A gallon of gas cost about twenty-five cents, but if my car went too far, I had to take up a collection to help pay for the gas. That old Pontiac didn't make it through the winter. I needed a new car. Dad went with me and I bought a brand new white Volkswagen, with the understanding I would pay him back as I did for the three hundred dollar Pontiac.

Dad had decided he didn't want to belong to the Church of the Brethren anymore because he felt they were always asking for money. His opinion was that the richest Protestant Church in Fort Wayne was the First Presbyterian Church on Wayne Street and therefore we started attending as a family. This was certainly not a Brethren Church that was very evident. Before the ten o'clock service on Sundays there was a coffee hour with coffee, doughnuts, juice and sweet rolls. Everyone stood around drinking and smoking and visiting.

First Presbyterian Church in Fort Wayne is very regal, almost cathedral like inside with tall round columns and a long aisle running between pews. It was rumored that a very prominent family owned their pew near the altar. Six people could fit into a pew and after you sat down on velvet seat cushions you shut the door. This was all very cozy and proper and strange to me. On special occasions like Christmas and Easter, there were French horns playing along with the pipe organ. I loved to go just to watch all the pomp.

My family joined this church after taking introductory classes, which I didn't attend since I was away in school. The Sunday we were accepted into this church community, we were called to the front of the church and each of us received a long stem red rose. All the years my family attended First Presbyterian my favorite thing was to sneak in late and sit in the foyer on Christmas Eve or New Years Eve. Most everyone sitting on folded chairs back there was a little too happy and far more interesting to watch. I never felt at home in this church but it is the church Zandra and Burnie remember. Mother had some friends but did not belong to any clubs or groups in this church like she had in Goshen.

Chapter 24

$\mathcal{A}$t Christmas break, Mother and I decided a big flocked tree for in this new house for the holidays would be nice. I had to pay for it. Dad would not. That Christmas on Ravenswood Drive, Mother invited two foreign students studying at Indiana Technical College to share our holiday dinner. This was all arranged through the church. Grandma and Grandpa Fogel joined us. Grandpa Gump remarried almost immediately after Grandma died. My father really resented that and I only saw Grandpa Gump a few times after Grandma died. His new wife was named Bertha and she surprisingly resembled my grandmother.

Mother wanted a full house for the holiday so she invited the foreign students. They were Muslims from Iran (Persia) and did not celebrate Christmas, but they were eager to visit in an American home. Dad had to go pick them up because neither had a car. Ali was very tall and dark. Ahmad was shorter, thin, and not as dark and wore glasses. They spoke English, but not really well. The dinner was a success. Everyone had a good time. When it was time to take Ali and Ahmad home, Ali asked if he could write to me at college so I gave him my address.

Every time Ali wrote to me he sent me a card with a rose on it. Sometimes it was a "thinking of you" card, sometimes a "get well" card or even a "sympathy" card. I don't think he knew the difference but they all had roses on them. I came home about twice a month and would have a date with Ali. I would pick him up at Indiana Tech after his last class and we would go to a movie and then to McDonald's for a strawberry milk shake. McDonald's was just new in Fort Wayne. If I had to baby-sit Zandra and Burnie, I would go get Ali and he would watch TV with me. I was very flattered by all this attention but it was going too fast for me. I was overwhelmed by his intense joy at being with me and a little scared. However, I continued seeing him until late spring. Then one night outside

McDonald's he said he wanted to marry me. That did it. I was scared me to death. The next time I was in town, I called him and met him in the parking lot of the Hobby House Restaurant downtown and told him I was going to marry someone else. He just stood there with his head hanging down trying to figure out what went wrong. We just had a big communication problem and I was too inexperienced to tell him.

School was going well. If it hadn't been for Ali, I would have happily stayed at school and gone home only when the dorm closed for holidays. As summer vacation was looming on the horizon, I wanted to go home less and less. Dad was building a new house for the family, but he was not mending his ways. Both Mother and Dad were never happy it seemed. Mother had found a teaching job for the next fall 1961 at Irwin School on the south side of Fort Wayne. She was just about finished with her bachelor's degree.

I decided to go to summer school. Jean and I and a couple of other friends rented the basement apartment on Manitou Lake in Rochester, Indiana about ten miles west of North Manchester. The sheriff from Peru and his family were renting the main floor of this cottage for two weeks. We were there for a month. Every weekday I drove the four of us girls into Manchester and we attended classes. Summer school was very relaxed and I liked it. Besides at the end of the day we could go home to the lake. We did most of our studying while on campus waiting for our roommates to finish with their classes. Then when we were at the lake we were able to just have fun.

Our classes lasted for six weeks, so I had to drive back and forth from home in Fort Wayne a couple of weeks after our month at the lake were over. The rest of the summer I stayed at home. It seems like everyone was walking on tiptoe. No one wanted to upset Dad and it didn't take much. Mom was so busy finishing her college degree and getting ready for the new job. She didn't grow any flowers nor have a garden. Some of my friends from school came over a couple of times. Carol was a favorite of

Mother's. Carol would help Mother in the kitchen and they talked about hairstyles and clothes. Mother didn't like Jean and Gail as much. They weren't as gossipy.

In the fall of 1961, Mother started teaching at Irwin School and I started my last year on campus at Manchester. I was a junior. Gail, Jean and I didn't want to live in a dorm so we rented a bedroom with kitchen privileges from Elaine, a divorced mother with three kids.

In the spring of 1962, Dad moved the family into the house he had built on Orlando Drive in Ludwig Park on the northwest corner of Fort Wayne. He waited until school was over so Mom had more time. This house was bigger than the house on Ravenswood Drive. The living room was big enough for the piano and Zandra and Burnie started taking lessons. Mother was determined one of her kids would learn to play the piano. She used to tell me if I learned to play the piano I would be the most popular girl in college.

We settled in and I felt at home as much as possible. I took two classes that summer and had to drive from home in Fort Wayne to school every day. After those classes, I was finished with my college work on campus. Because of all the summer classes I had taken I had nearly enough credits to graduate after three years.

Dad became more erratic. He found out he was diabetic and this man, who was never sick, just could not handle a chronic disease. He never remembered to, or would not, take his pills. He passed out one night, at a local gas station trying to get a bottle of pop from the machine because his blood sugar was low. The ambulance was called and he was taken to the hospital. When Dad's blood sugar was under control, he was sent home.

One time later that summer Dad came home and threatened to shoot himself. He went out in the backyard and fired his little gun with the mother of pearl handle. Mother called the police. Dad was put back in

Lutheran Hospital and given a battery of tests. He was found to be paranoid. Today, he probably would have been considered bi-polar and would have received medication.

Mother was now teaching at St. Joe School on St. Joe Road. It was a country school and she fit right in and loved it. Zandra and Burnie went to school on the bus to Washington Center School, which ironically was originally Wallen School where Mother taught when I was very little. I started my student teaching in that school in September of 1962. I also needed to pick up some history credits so I attended a history class at Indiana University Extension in downtown Fort Wayne. I spent many evenings in the Allen County library studying just to get out of the house. Dad often followed me and I had no idea why.

On a very cold and icy night that winter, I took Zandra and Burnie to see "101 Dalmatians" at the Embassy Theater. Mom and Dad had gone to see a movie at some other theater. I had to park my car in a parking lot and we walked across the street to the movie. Somehow between the ticket booth and the ticket taker, Burnie lost his ticket. I had to buy him another one and it took the last of my money. I didn't have enough left to get the car out of the parking lot. All through the movie I worried about what to do because I was unable to reach our parents. Finally I called Aunt Marie from the theater lobby and she drove past the theater with her window rolled down and handed me some money. I swore I would never take my siblings to another movie.

I finished my student teaching right before Christmas and started looking for a job one semester before the rest of my class back at Manchester. Jean's father was a trustee in Adams County, Decatur. He knew they needed a kindergarten teacher at Monmouth School and told me to apply. I did and I got the job, which began in late January 1963. I told my parents I needed to live on the south side of Ft. Wayne, so I could get out of their house and away from all the turbulence. I rented an apartment in an old house on Wildwood near the old Lutheran Hospital. I don't emember where I got the money for the first month's rent, probably from Mom, but I moved in before school began. The Monmouth kindergarten was a new adventure for that school. I started their first kindergarten and it was in an old dairy building about a mile from the school. I had two groups of five-year-old students. I enjoyed every minute. At night I drove my little white VW back to my apartment. The apartment was small. The bed was in the living room and there was a nice kitchen and bath. The elderly couple who owned this house locked the front door every night at 11:00 so I was never out late.

Back home things were getting worse. I was not there so I missed much of it. Mother filed for divorce and Dad was almost beyond being rational at the thought of losing his family. Mother finally had a restraining order against him to keep him away from the family. But he still showed up often threatening physical harm or making outlandish promises. Many nights Mother, Zandra and Burnie stayed at the Travel Lodge in downtown Ft. Wayne so Dad couldn't find them.

Late in May of 1963, I graduated from Manchester College with my class even though I had been teaching since January. I went over to Manchester the night before and stayed in East Hall Dorm with my friends. Graduation was in the auditorium the next day. A tradition at Manchester College was for the graduates to file out after the ceremony and make a big circle on the knoll of lawn holding hands and singing the school song. By the time that was over all families and friends were outside and everyone headed for their family groups. I stood there alone. I walked back to East Hall, picked up my overnight bag and drove my VW back to Fort Wayne. Mother took me to see the movie "Hud" and out to dinner. I don't remember where Dad was, or if he even knew.

I packed up my stuff and moved out of my apartment. I was only home for a few days. Gail was getting married in July. Her mother was not well and they needed help. They asked me to come and stay with them until the wedding. I was maid of honor. I moved to Gail's house for about six weeks. They had a lovely house on the edge of Crown Point not far from Chicago but still in Indiana. Gail's father was one of the directors of U.S. Steel, Gary Works. He had a big office with his own bathroom at the plant. Their house was built on a cliff and the back yard was terraced in high steps which Gail's mother wanted planted with flowers so the yard would be lovely for the outside wedding reception. We spent hours every day shopping for plants and then planting them. Everything had to be perfect for the reception.

Even with all the work, Gail and I found time to read. Also, I was beginning to walk in the evenings to try to keep my weight under control. Now I weighed two hundred and ten pounds. We went to movies. We even found time to swim in the Gary Country Club pool. A lot of time was spent on the wedding dress and bridesmaids' dresses. Mine had to be handmade. Yellow orchids were ordered from Hawaii. We went into Chicago and Gail picked out her china and registered at Marshall Fields and other places. Invitations were addressed and sent out. We helped her mother make gifts for the servers.

On the day of the wedding it rained hard all day. The photographer still took some beautiful pictures with colorful umbrellas and raindrops, but she dropped the camera and most of the pictures were lost. The summer yard reception was now in the house and no one enjoyed all our hard work on the terrace. The bartender from the Gary Country Club was set up in the garage. My Mother and Zandra came and were duly impressed with the entire Crown Point and Gary social crowd.

Chapter 25

On September 1963, I was promoted to teach first grade at Monmouth School. I prepared for this new experience and looked for a new apartment. Dad showed up at the house often. He was supposed to be living elsewhere but couldn't accept that the family, and especially Mother, could live without him. We tried to deal with our everyday lives and pretend all was normal. Dad was mentally ill but that knowledge didn't help when he threatened my mother. When my friend Carol got married and went on a long honeymoon, she let Mother, Zandra and Burnie stay in her apartment just to get away from Dad.

I rented a downstairs apartment in Ft. Wayne, one half block from Memorial Park, just on the edge of the "questionable neighborhoods." There was one big bedroom with a large walk-in closet, a narrow kitchen with a bath off to the side of it, and a living room in front. I used the back door because it was closer to the alley where I parked my VW. I buried myself with my move. I made flash cards and fixed things for bulletin boards and wrote up lesson plans for school, so I didn't have to think about what was going on at home. School didn't start until after Labor Day.

One day Dad asked me to meet him at the Churubusco Bank to set up a loan for me so I could pay him off for my VW. He was pleasant and we chatted about my teaching job. That was the last time I saw my father alive. I was not quite twenty three years old.

On the night of September 12, 1963, Dad drove his brand new Roadmaster Buick with the wooden dashboard behind St. Joe Public School and parked so it could be seen from Mother's classroom window. He then took a long vacuum hose, from a house he was building, and attached one end to the exhaust pipe and the other end inserted into the driver's side vent window. He started the car, and it was still running the next morning when Mother's principal found the car with Dad dead inside.

I was already at school when my principal told me I was to leave and go home. He wouldn't tell me why, but I knew. I had had a dream during the night that my friend Ahmad had died in a plane crash and I woke up crying. I knew the emergency was not Ahmad but Dad and I knew he was dead. There was such a sense of relief when I arrived home. Dad was safe now and so were we.

The funeral was at the First Presbyterian Church. Dad was buried in Lindenwood Cemetery. Dad was only forty-eight years old. He accomplished so much in his life and had so much yet to live for. His only son was ten years old and Zandra was thirteen. Dad couldn't deal with mental or physical illness and the medical community or his family were unable to be of much help. We didn't understand what to do and there was no one to help us to understand. His doctor later told Mother he was thankful Dad only killed himself and not all of us. What a terrible thing to say to his widow. But now we could all breathe easier. Dad was not out there in the dark anymore.

Mother had a very hard time after Dad died. He had apparently lived off and on with a woman named Marjorie. She had been to the viewing at the funeral home and signed her first name in the guest book. She started calling every couple of days or so, never said anything, but we all knew who it was. After several weeks, mother told her Herbert would not be dead if it hadn't been for her. She never called again. Mother wanted to find this woman and had her friends take her to bars every weekend looking for her. They never found her. Mother also lost some of her memory over all this anxiety and stress. And then in November of 1963, President Kennedy was killed and the entire country went into a tailspin.

I was teaching first grade at Monmouth School. The principal announced over the PA system that President Kennedy had been shot and it didn't look good. Minutes later the announcement came that he was dead. No prayers were allowed in public schools, but we prayed for the President's family in my classroom. We finished school that day and did not go back until the next week. Everyone mourned. We were all glued to our TV sets.

Chapter 26

Grandpa Gump died of Parkinson's disease in March 1964. He had been in a nursing home for some time. Mother and I went to New Paris for his funeral and to the church on the banks of the Eel River where he was buried beside Grandma. It was almost like the closing of a door on the Gump family. I didn't see much of them for a long time.

Mother was settling down and she put her heart into her schoolwork. She was sure I would move home after Dad died. I had other ideas. Independence was not something I wanted to give up. Grandma Fogel didn't like me driving so far to work and called me after school every time the weather was bad. She was afraid I would have car trouble and be left stranded in the middle of nowhere. And of course she worried about Mother living alone without a man in the house. In her mind and in Mother's mind, a woman needed a man or she was not complete. They both should have known better because they were both independent women in unhappy marriages.

My principal and boss at Monmouth School was John McConaha. He was a very stern man with a volatile temper. He frightened me. He picked on me because I was new and easy to pick on. Monmouth School at that time was kindergarten through high school. Elementary teachers had to take their turn selling tickets at basketball games for the high school. I had always been bad at making change under pressure. I was shaking the entire evening when I had to sit in the little booth and sell tickets for the game. Then the principal locked me in his office with him as he counted the money after the game. I just knew I would be short about twenty dollars and have to make up the difference. Thank God, I was over by one dollar and he let me out.

When summer came I went to New Mexico. Jean and I decided to start our master's degrees at New Mexico State University in Las Cruces. Gail and her husband Philip lived in an apartment in LasCruces. Gail arranged for Jean and me to live with a lady from Belgium. We each had our own room and kitchen privileges, but we were rarely there as we were always on the go. Philip, Gail, Jean and I spent every Saturday or Sunday traveling around visiting ghost towns, silver mines, Indian sights and White Sands National Park. Jean and I ate out nearly every evening. This was our first encounter with Mexican food. No one back home had even heard of tacos or corn dogs but we became very familiar with them.

Gail, Jean and I drove my VW to the Mexican border a couple of times. We parked in El Paso and walked into Juarez. I bought Mother a kangaroo skin purse. I bought two pearl and ruby rings, one for Zandra and one for myself. I bought Burnie a huge sombrero and other Mexican trinkets. We watched glass blowers and I bought six hand-blown amber glasses. Of course then I had to buy a hand woven basket with leather handles in which to carry the glasses. We caught a cab and drove around town to see what it was like away from the market at the border. Mud is what I remember.

Summer classes came to an end and Jean and I headed back to Indiana. My little VW overflowed with gifts and souvenirs. Back in Indiana I dropped Jean at her parents' house near Decatur and I went on to Mom's on Orlando Drive in Fort Wayne where I stayed until I found another apartment.

In the fall of 1964, I rented an apartment just off South Clinton in Fort Wayne. So far, I had rented only furnished apartments, so it wasn't hard to move often. Burnie helped me make a bookcase. I was reading a lot of books and easily filled the shelves. That fall, I enrolled at Saint Francis College in Fort Wayne to continue work on my master's degree. I had to have a masters' degree to get an Indiana Life Teachers License. Since it looked like I would be teaching forever, I knew I better get on with it. I took only one class a semester during the school year and two classes in the summers.

I taught first grade at Monmouth School until 1970. It was a joy to see the light go on in children's eyes when they understood what I taught them. I had fun teaching first graders and I did a lot of fun projects with my students. We made a teepee out of brown packaging paper and drew Indian symbols on it. This teepee was big enough for two to three children to sit inside and read. We made a circus train out of cardboard boxes for favorite stuffed animals from home to ride in and to make up stories about. John, the principal, and I were even getting along better after I taught two of his own children. I acquired more self-confidence and was able to stand up to him on occasion.

The best part of teaching for me was to teach children to read. I had had such problems with reading myself and had found later in life the joy of reading so I wanted to impart that joy to young minds. In the 60's, children in general did not attend kindergarten, especially country children. So many of my students came to me not knowing we read left to right or not knowing any of the letters of the alphabet. Many could not write their names or use scissors. What a sense of worthwhile accomplishment I had at the end of the year when I looked at my class and remembered where they had been in September and how far they had come by May. No profession could fit me better.

At home, my life revolved around preparing for students at Monmouth and taking classes at St. Francis. Two Monmouth High School teachers lived near me and paid me to drive them to school every day. I taught reading and math in summer school every summer for six years in grades three to six. I started teaching summer school because it was just in the mornings and I needed the extra money for graduate school. So I taught school in the mornings and went to classes in the afternoon and evenings.

As a treat for myself, I bought a pet. Dad could not take it away this time. She was a Siamese cat I named Kismet. Jean went with me and

I picked her out of a litter of six. I paid fifteen dollars for Kismet and put her in my coat pocket. She hid safely in there while we made a grocery store stop to get her condensed milk. Kismet would prove to be one of the best things I ever did for myself.

I also bought a new car that year. The VW had seen me through many tough times and we had traveled many miles together. Dad went with me when I bought the VW. I really missed him when it came time to buy a new car. On the other hand, he never would have approved of the car I bought. Everyone needs to buy a car just for fun once in their lives and that's what I did. I bought a white Corvair convertible with baby blue interior and I thought I was hot stuff!

Chapter 27

$\mathcal{M}$other started dating. She was like a kid in a candy store. She was very naïve about men. My problems with my mother started at this time and lasted for many years to come as in many ways our lives became parallel. She kind of lost sight of her family and went about life having fun. Maybe she deserved it after the stress of so many years with Dad. But on the other hand, she had two children at home and she was not always a good example to them.

Mother dated a man named Richard for over a year. We all liked him very much. He took Burnie fishing and did things around the house. He took Mom dancing which she loved. The only problem was that Richard was married. He never lied about it. He was a salesman and traveled all through states near his home base in Chicago. His wife lived in Chicago and they were not close, so he said. However, he made it clear he would not be getting a divorce.

Another of Mom's male friends was Charles. He was well to do and retired, his wife was dead and he wanted to marry Mother. She wasn't interested. Mother wanted to have fun. She did not want to take care of an old man. Charles bought Zandra and me lovely gifts like real hairpieces and pearl bracelets. Mother and Charles were friends a long time.

There were other men in and out over the next several years and I disapproved because Burnie and Zandra were still in the house. I felt she left them alone too much and having men in and out was not proper for a mother of teenagers. We had many heated talks during this time. Zandra came and stayed with me once in awhile. Mother got into the habit of calling me about how to parent Zandra who was now fifteen. If Mom thought Zan was wearing too much makeup, Mother would call and ask me about it. Again I felt like I was part their mother as well as their sister. I was not comfortable with that position in my life.

During Christmas vacation I read a nonfiction book by Dr. Wayne Dyer. It was about taking control of your life and losing weight. It really hit home for me. On New Year's Eve I went with Aunt Marie and Uncle Frank to a New Year's Eve Party at St. Mary's Catholic Church. The next day, January 1, 1966, I started my own diet without any doctor. I was determined to be a normal sized woman. The first step was to inform Mother I would not be home for any family dinners until the dishes were done. Every time I walked into her house I headed for comfort food. That behavior was ingrained in me and it had to stop.

My diet was simple. I drank a can of Metecale (similar to Slim Fast) for breakfast and a small glass of grapefruit juice. I ate no lunch. I stayed at my desk and graded papers and got lots of work accomplished instead of eating. When I got home from school around 4:30, I ate a salad consisting of half a head of lettuce, one package of slender sliced beef and a dressing of vinegar and oil. All evening I drank two quarts of unsweetened Kool-Aid. I ate that every day. Every time I lost ten pounds, Jean and I went to the Gashouse restaurant for a proper dinner. As time went by and I lost a lot of weight, I added sugar free fruit and eggs and cottage cheese instead of the salad a couple of times a week.

Grandpa Fogel died that same January. He had been in the hospital a week or so and I had visited him. Mother told me he was afraid to die because he felt he had not lived a good life. He died on January 19, 1966 of heart problems. He was 82 years old and I felt like I never knew who he really was. He was a quiet man and of course never talked about his feelings. He worked hard all his life but never seemed to get anywhere. Grandpa's funeral was in the church beside their house in Huntertown with the big family dinner afterwards. Grandma told me to go over to the church and take one of the vases of flowers home. I took the pure white vase with red carnations and a red velvet bow. I still have that red velvet ribbon and I used it on my front door for many Christmas holiday seasons.

By October of 1966, I had lost eighty pounds and for months men had been flirting with me. These were not college boys far from their homes. These were good old red-blooded American men and I was even more naïve than my mother was when it came to men. Now my problems really began with men. I had never dated in high school or college. The only men I had known used me as a friend, a tutor or as someone to iron their shirts. I didn't know how to play the dating games most girls grew up knowing.

Over the months when I was lost weight, I needed new clothes and I went to K-Mart and bought a few dresses. Women only wore dresses to work. By October when I reached my ideal weight, I had saved some money for good clothes and Mother gave me one hundred dollars for losing all that weight. Two hundred dollars could go a long way in the sixties. The one person I knew who was knowledgeable about good clothes and fashion was Gail's mother. They now lived in Pittsburgh. So Gail and I drove in my white convertible to Pittsburgh and spent two days shopping with her mother. I wore size 12, a long way from the size 22 I had worn the year before. Size 12 was considered the perfect size. What fun I had! I bought dresses and skirts and sweater sets and suits and even some jewelry. Gail's mother even gave me a dress and matching coat she could no longer wear. I returned to my Columbia Avenue apartment in Fort Wayne with a car full of lovely things and memories of a fabulous shopping trip.

Jean worked in Fort Wayne now. She rented an apartment across the street from me on Columbia Avenue. Jean was a magnet for friends. Many of us would get together on Wednesday and Friday nights and go out to dance clubs. This was another entirely new life for me. I was always asked to dance and I made lots of friends. But somehow I was so naïve, I never thought about married men being out there on the dating scene. Guys would ask me out and then after a couple of dates tell me they were married. I couldn't handle it. All my life I had tried so hard to please everyone so they would like me and now I didn't know how to say, "Get out of my life." I had some very unpleasant experiences before I got the hang of it.

That summer, Jean and I rented a cabin on Crooked Lake in the lake country north of Fort Wayne for one week. Mom, Zandra and Burnie were renting it the week after us. It was a nice get away from all the stuff at home. I asked Zandra to stay with us a couple of days. The three of us went to the theater in Angola and saw the movie, "The Apartment." Zan sat in the seat next to the aisle. During the movie, the man who had sat there for the previous showing came and asked Zan to stand so he could search the seat. He was on vacation with his family and had lost his billfold. He searched. Found nothing. Pretty soon he was back with theater personnel and a flashlight and they searched. And again found nothing. This was repeated one more time and finally they found his billfold wedged down in the back of the seat. That was the end of taking my sister to a movie.

I graduated from St. Francis College that spring of 1967. I now had a Masters Degree in Elementary Education majoring in Reading. The scared, fat, crippled little kid who was so afraid of reading was now able to teach other young children how much fun reading could be. Never did a child have to stand up to read in one of my classes unless they wanted to. For graduation, I wore a colorful striped dress with a wide patent leather belt. The dress had been Zandra's and I liked it so well she let me wear it. Mother and Zandra were at my graduation, but I never saw them. They left early because they both had a date that evening. Jean took me to the Gashouse for dinner.

One of the places all the young adults, supposedly unmarried ones, hung out was "The Apartment," a bar dance club on the south side of Fort Wayne. My girlfriends and I were there every Wednesday night and maybe on Friday night. Then on Saturday nights there was usually a party someplace. I was getting a little better with men. I now dated a divorced man, David. He was an engineer at International Harvester. He took me out to dinner a few times, but most of the time he would show up and just plan to watch my TV for the evening. That was to become the way it went for awhile until I learned to kick these dead beats out of my life. I was now 27 years old. Grandma Fogel was so afraid I would never get married. She spent many hours worrying about me being an old maid. She also thought I was too thin because my collarbones showed. I was delighted my bones showed and wore a pearl in the hollow of my throat on purpose.

Jean and I were getting so discouraged with the men we met, we decided we needed a change. And since we were together much of the time, we decided to rent a really nice unfurnished apartment together. Turtle Creek was a brand new apartment complex on Paulding Road on the south side of Fort Wayne. We rented a two bedroom apartment in the newest building next to the club house and pools. Since this apartment was not furnished we bought some cheap furniture and moved in the fall of 1967. That first winter we nearly froze to death. Something was wrong with the heating system and we sat around in coats for several days until they fixed it. Jean's father had a full-length raccoon coat from his youth and we made good use of it.

At home, Mother still dated. Zandra and Burnie were in high school. Zandra had spent a summer in Europe with a touring American High School Choir. Mom was sure Zandra was going to be the daughter I was not. Zandra did not have a weight problem. She had natural curly blond hair, albeit she was always trying to iron it straight. Mother sent her to finishing school. She was entered into some beauty contests. It was all lighthearted fun, but I think Mom took it pretty seriously. I still didn't spend much time at home. Mom got on my nerves. When I would call her looking for some sympathy or motherly encouragement, I only heard about the latest boyfriend. It got to the point I didn't even call.

Jean joined the Tall Club of Fort Wayne. You had to be over a certain height to belong. She easily made it, but of course I wasn't in the club. They did meet in our apartment sometimes and decided to make me their mascot since I was only five feet tall. We still went out to clubs and were dating different guys off and on. Kismet was still with me and a great comfort. So far she had broken the record as my longest lasting pet. I started getting my hair professionally done every week. I had a beautiful hair style with big flat curls high on top of my head and corkscrew curls beside my ears.

One truth I do know, being overweight was a far bigger handicap to me, as a young woman, than having polio. People often tend to be kind and accept a handicapped person. On the other hand, people tend to be very unkind and think of an overweight person as inferior. And another truth I know is about words. The word "crippled" has a meaning to people like me that is derogatory. To me it means, lazy, unable to care for yourself and unwilling to try. Handicapped means you are a normal person with a problem you are handling. Crippled is an old-fashioned word and was replaced with handicapped with an updated meaning. The Shriner's Hospital even changed its name from Shriner's Crippled Children's Hospital to Shriner's Children's Hospital. Words do make a difference.

Chapter 28

$\mathcal{M}$other began dating Bob Craig. He was just another man around and I didn't think too much about him. He worked for the railroad and was divorced. He had at least six children and was Catholic. Zandra was at Purdue by now and Mother was very impressed with her friends. Mom went to Lafayette to see Zandra at college more often than she came to see me across town.

Through the Tall Club, Jean met Earl. She started dating him steadily in 1968. And by late fall they decided to get married after the holidays. I could not afford to live at Turtle Creek by myself, so I was on the move again. This time I rented a ground level apartment on Beaver Avenue. Being handicapped was not something I thought about all the time. But I had to live on the first floor so I could carry in groceries and such. It was not always easy to find a ground floor apartment.

Jean, Judy, Sue and Phylis were the group of girls I went out with. Phylis, Judy and Jean all worked together. They all had dates for New Year's Eve so I was planning a quiet New Year's Eve at home that year. It surely was not the first time I would be alone with Kismet on New Year's Eve. Then Phylis called. Her boyfriend, Tom, had a friend who needed a date for New Year's Eve. So a blind date was set and I wasn't expecting much.

They all came together and picked me up, Tom, Phylis and Dan. When I opened the door, I thought, "Well at least this guy is really cute." Dan was a skydiver and so we went to a skydiver's party at one of guy's homes. Tom was driving some old car that didn't have a heater and it was four below zero that night, but it was the beginning of the rest of my life. Dan was a genuine gentleman. He always treated me like a lady. He never showed up with a six pack and took over the TV. Our second date he called and asked me to go to a movie two days in advance! We saw "Camelot" and then we went to The Apartment for a drink after the movie. Dan was kind, thoughtful and not afraid of his intelligence or voicing his religious beliefs. We knew all the same people and I had no idea why we hadn't met before. We fell into a routine. He would call on Wednesday and ask me out for Saturday.

Jean and Earl married in January and I was maid of honor. I asked Dan to be my date at Jean's reception. My mother met him there and she later called him a pip squeak because he didn't weigh much more than I did. He had not been back from Vietnam very long. While in Vietnam for thirteen months, he earned several medals including the Purple Heart and the Commendation of Valor. Dan came from a very Catholic family and was a high school graduate. I came from a very Protestant family and had a Master's degree. I am also six years older. Dan and I soon started going out twice a week, Wednesday nights and Saturday nights. He took me home to meet his mother. One thing we had in common was that both our fathers were dead. His had died when Dan was only five.

One Saturday that winter, I went out to visit with Mom. She told me she and Bob had decided to get married. I must have had a strange look on my face because she went on to say he had a good job and he showered twice a day. I thought that was no reason to get married. But they were married in March in the Chapel at the First Presbyterian Church. She ended up marrying and divorcing Bob twice. He was an alcoholic and Mother thought she could change him. She had always wanted to be Grandma Gump, but now she was Mrs. Craig and would never be Grandma Gump.

Everyone around me was getting married. I was twenty-eight years old and I really didn't care if I got married or not. I knew very few people who were happily married and I wasn't sure I even wanted to try. But when Dan brought me home after a date on his birthday, June 21, he asked me to marry him and I knew it was right so I said yes. I loved him and I knew he really loved me. He gave me the ring his mother had told him he could have when he got married. It was his grandmother's engagement ring and it fit me perfectly. We have always thought that God had a hand in bringing us together.

We set a date for in October. Dan's uncle, Monsignor William Faber was the priest at Queen of Angels Catholic Church in Fort Wayne. He would marry us. With a date set, and plans begun, we had to tell Grandmother Fogel I was going to marry a Catholic. Grandma had mellowed as she aged. She now needed a walker to get around and didn't leave the house too often. In warm weather, she sat on her front porch and watched her neighbors. She became more tolerant of others. Grandma was so happy I finally found someone who was willing to marry me; she didn't care if Dan was Catholic.

On October 18, 1969, Daniel Patrick O'Brien and I married at Queen of Angels Catholic Church on State Street. Burnie, who was sixteen, gave me away. I'm sure Burnie was happy he would never have to move me to a new apartment again. Zandra was my maid of honor and my only bride's maid. We had a small wedding with only family present, with the exception of Phylis. She took full responsibly for our marriage since she introduced us and insisted on being at our wedding. Dan's brother was his best man. Mrs. Cherry made my dress of cream colored satin. She also made Zandra's dress which was a floor length burnt orange gown. I carried a cascading bouquet of burnt orange mums. The men all wore brown tuxedoes. It was a pretty autumn wedding and the day was chilly with a brilliant blue sky. The reception was right after the wedding at a north side motel. It was very simple with beer, coffee, soft drinks, nuts, cake and ice cream. Mother paid to have my dress made and that's all she paid toward my wedding. She had just married Bob a few months before and didn't want to spend money on me.

The day before the wedding, Mother asked me if I had told Dan I could not have children. I was struck dumb. What did she mean? What about all those lectures she had delivered about "it only takes one night to

ruin the rest of your life?" She now said she thought I could not have children because of polio. She had just thought that up, no doctor had ever
mentioned it to her and it made no sense to me. So I just ignored her and
went on with my life.

I had been sick with a bad cold the week before the wedding and I
was still not well. All the stress of the wedding and teaching school had
done me in. I probably had bronchitis, but I didn't go to the doctor. I was
afraid he would put me in the hospital. Mother had some strong cough
syrup with codeine. I kept the little bottle in my hand during the wedding
in case I started coughing, which I did.

We spent our first night in a motel in Franklin, Indiana just outside
Indianapolis. I coughed so much all night that I was afraid Dan would have
second thoughts about this marriage. The next day we arrived at the old
hotel in French Lick, Indiana, a very plush and old-fashioned grand hotel
best known for its sulfur springs. We received a small complimentary bottle of champagne. After we shared the bottle, Dan wrapped me up in a
blanket and I slept for hours while he watched football on TV. The next day
I felt better and we enjoyed the rest of our week. After a few days in the
elegance of French Lick, we spent a day or two in Nashville, Indiana,
which is an artist colony and the place to visit each fall in Indiana.

Monday came too soon and we both went back to work. Dan was
a steelworker at Joslyn Stainless Steels in Fort Wayne. Married life was
great. We lived in my old apartment on Beaver Street. Dan was easy to
cook for because he ate most anything except sweets. Kismet didn't like
him at all. She loved high places and sat on the high windowsills above our
bed. During the night she would jump down on our bed and Dan would
nearly have a heart attack. Another place she liked was on top of the refrigerator. Dan once reached up there to pick her up and she bit him hard on
the hand leaving four puncture marks. And yet he stayed with me and did-
n't give up or make me chose between Kismet or him. I loved Dan then
and after all these years, our marriage continues to be strong and healthy.

*"April 17, 1938
Marjorie and
Herbert's Wedding"*

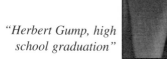

*"Herbert Gump, high
school graduation"*

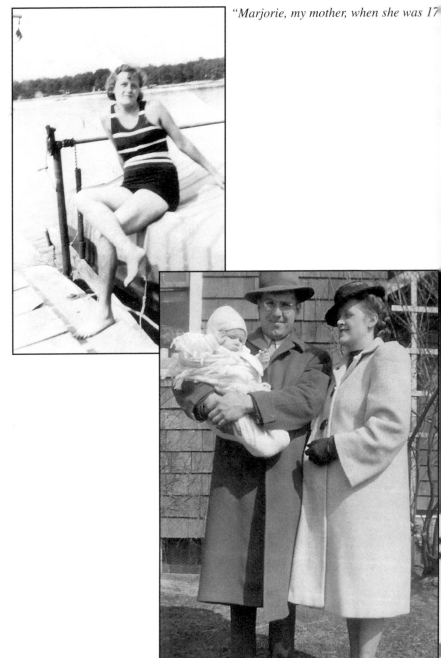

"Marjorie, my mother, when she was 17"

"Easter Sunday 1941. Herbert and Marjorie with six-month old Roxann"

*"Charles and Gertrude Gump...
1954. My Gump grandparents"*

"Emma Mae and Sidney Fogel sitting with me...1964. My Fogel grandparents"

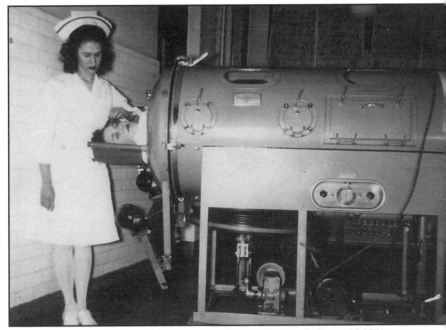

"Iron Lung, St. Joe Hospital, Fort Wayne, Indiana 1946"

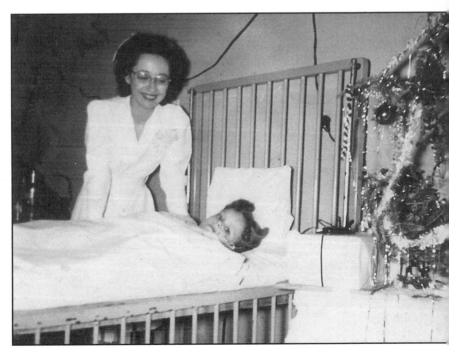

"Miss Kinzer standing beside me after I was removed from the iron lung"

"With a friend in California on the pig ranch. I am wearing my leg brace right before Dad removed it."

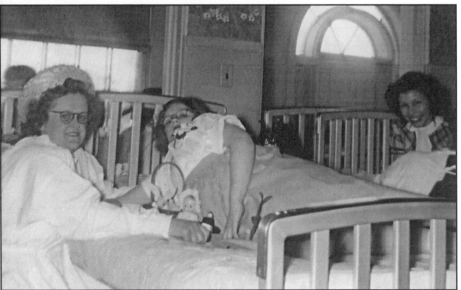

"Shriners...Easter Sunday and parents are visiting. I am in my body cast and cannot sit."

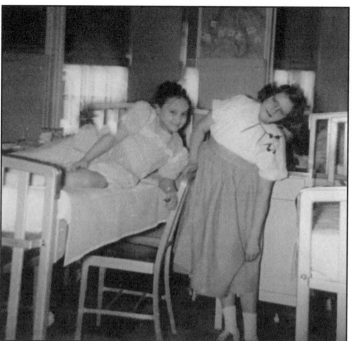

"Shriners Hospital. Mother brought me a gardenia to wear while she was visiting I am in my body cast and the wedgings are well underway.'

"1958 Christmas card picture with Zandra, Burnie and me."

"August 1963, my family just weeks before Dad died."

"My engagement picture, 1969"

"October 18, 1969 Dan and I married. Grandma Fogel is standing with us."

"My three children in 1977; Mike, Rachel and Carrie."

"Rachel's eighth grade graduation 1991. Rachel, Mike, me, Dan and Carrie."

"Dan and I, Christmas 2001"

"Christmas 2001, Burnell, Mother, me and Zandra"

"*June 4, 2002 Mother's 87th birthday party. One month before she died.*"

"*May 2000, I am on my first outing in my new power wheelchair.*"

Chapter 29

*M*arried only a few months, Dan and I started talking about having children. I was with kids all day so therefore I really didn't care if I had children, but we talked it over and decided to try. We now started looking for a house to buy. We spent several weeks visiting houses in different parts of Fort Wayne. We never found the house where we felt we could raise our family. Then the realtor told us about a house in the small town of Zanesville ten miles south of Fort Wayne. The house was so much bigger and cleaner than anything we had looked at in our price range in the city. We bought this four-bedroom, two-story house in March of 1970 for twenty-five thousand dollars. The previous owners raised their three children there and had taken loving care of the one hundred-year-old house. I had not lived in a two-story house more than a few months since I was very small. I was looking forward to this new adventure. Dan had never lived in a small town since his family was from Chicago and Fort Wayne. He was in for some surprises.

Mother now stepped in. She thought we didn't know what we were doing. She couldn't believe we would buy an old house and she not only disapproved but she insisted on seeing it. So we took her out and she met the owners and went through the house. She agreed it was a good house, she liked the owners and how they had maintained the property, but she was concerned about how I would make it up and down the stairs to the bedrooms and to the basement. I assured her I would manage.

Mom's life was not going as she had expected. Burnie wasn't happy living there with her and Bob. But the good part was Zandra was marrying a doctor's son. Mom's dream was if we couldn't marry a doctor, at least marry his son. Bruce told Mom he would pay for the rest of Zandra's college if Mom allowed her to marry before she graduated from Purdue. It was agreed. They married in August of 1970 and moved to New

Jersey where Bruce had a job while working on a master's degree in New York City. Zandra finished college while they lived in the East.

We moved into our new home that summer. Several of our friends including Phylis and Tom helped us move in. Our families gave us furniture they wanted to get off their hands now that we had the biggest house. I did buy new appliances and living room sofa and chair. Our house had a full basement and attic. We settled in and sort of rattled around in all those rooms for a while.

Dan and I slowly adjusted to small town living. I continued driving to Decatur every day to work. With both of us gone most of the time, we didn't make a lot of friends in Zanesville. But everyone seemed to know all about us. In no time at all, neighbors were calling Dan, "Danny." He was not used to such familiarity from strangers. We had to pick up our mail at the post office, and still do. The postmistress was not overly friendly, but knew us by sight and, of course, knew what mail we received. Dan always took just a sandwich to work and one day he dropped the sandwich in the out going mailbox instead of a letter he was going to mail. He mailed the letter in Fort Wayne.

The first Thanksgiving in our new home, Dan's family was invited for dinner along with my mother and Grandma Fogel. We were somewhat worried because not only was Father Bill going to be there, but also a visiting priest from Ireland was coming. I kept remembering all the stories Grandma told me about how bad the Catholics were and here she would be dining with two Catholic priests. Grandma turned out to be great. She never knew a stranger and that held true when she came face to face with Catholic Priests. She talked their legs off and it is pretty hard to outtalk a priest, especially two of them. That was the only time Grandma came to our house. She never learned to drive and by that Thanksgiving she had to use a walker full time in order to walk around in her own house.

I decided to convert to the Catholic Church. Belief in God was mportant to me not the institution to which I belonged, although I believe churches serve a great need. If for no other reason, it was a place to go for one hour every week and meditate which otherwise is so easy to put off and never do. And I thought our family should all be the same religion. I had started instructions at church. The classes took nine months and started with the beginning of the Bible. Father Bill felt it was silly for me to take all those hours of classes when I was already a Christian and he said he would give me instructions instead, which he did in about three sessions. My first communion was at the Midnight Mass on Christmas Eve. Zandra, Bruce and my Mother sat in the second row behind Dan and me. I went up for communion and after we sat down, Father Carroll, the priest from Ireland, accidentally backed into a candle and started his robe on fire. Zandra wondered if the Catholic Church was always that exciting.

Burnie started his senior year of high school and he was having problems with his life. He left home just weeks before he was to graduate and hitch hiked out West. Mother and Bob were having problems. It was not an easy time at home. Burnie kept in touch with Mom and he finally came back home safe. He was able to get his high school diploma and started working for his girlfriend's dad doing construction work. Sandy and Burnie married soon after high school and rented a little house out in the country.

Mother and Bob were moving into Canterbury Green apartments. Bob didn't like living in a house my Dad had built. With all of us out of the house, Mom was willing to move. She gave Dan and me some furniture she couldn't use and stored many things in our attic. Again she started over in a new environment and life would be wonderful. Her optimistic attitude was always shining through.

The autumn after Dan and I were married my job changed. I was still in the same school system but the superintendent asked me to be the Remedial Reading teacher for all three North Adams elementary schools. I had an office in each building and drove from building to building during the school week. It was the perfect job. I did not have any of the busy work involved in teaching. I didn't do grades, didn't have to go to PTA meetings, only met with the parents I needed to see. It was great. I just taught reading and the joy of reading to children who were where I once was. I loved that job.

Every summer Dan's family went to Colorado. By the time I was part of this family, Colorado was Dan and his family's second home. However, the first summer Dan and I were married; we stayed home and went to Cedar Point in Ohio. The second year we flew to Newark, my first time in an airplane, and spent some time visiting Zandra and Bruce in their apartment in New Jersey. On July 4 that year, Bruce took us into New York to see the sights. Many people had left the city for the holiday and it was a good time to visit.

I had a miscarriage in May before we went to see Zandra. Later that summer we went to Colorado for my first trip out to meet all of Dan's Colorado family. I took another pregnancy test which took a couple of long, high anxiety days to get the results. I was pregnant!

We spent two weeks that August in Colorado and I had a hard time with Betsy, my mother-in-law and her sister Aunt Gert. They both talked at the same time to me when we were alone and never stopped. I didn't want to offend them and did not know which one to look at when they were both talking. So I bought some felt fabric and sewing things and started making a Christmas tree skirt; that way I could sew and nod my head and didn't have to look at either one.

Back in Indiana, Grandma Fogel was thrilled I was pregnant. When we were first married, she allowed Dan and me to make a garden in her backyard. She urged us to run the rows of vegetables parallel to the street so her neighbors wouldn't see how crooked our rows were. Dan and I got into the habit of visiting her every couple of Saturdays or so to hoe and weed and visit. One Saturday in October we found her not feeling well and I helped her get undressed and into bed. I was surprised how frail she was when I helped her undress. After she was in bed, I called my mother and Aunt Marie. We stayed a little while until she was asleep and then we left knowing her daughters were on their way. Grandma was hospitalized that night and died a couple days later. She was 86 years old and alert to the end. Her funeral was on our second wedding anniversary. She was buried beside Grandpa in the cemetery on the Gump Road just east of Huntertown. She was never able to meet my first born but she knew he was eagerly expected.

Chapter 30

I taught until the end of the first semester in January 1972 and then took a leave of absence until the next fall so I could have my baby. Our baby was due in early April and I was taking it slow fixing up the nursery and looking forward to baby showers. I had plenty of time. But Mike had other ideas. He was born February 9, two months early and weighted only 3.6 pounds. In 1972 babies that small often didn't live. The pediatrician told me not to mail out announcements for a few days. Mike never lost weight like most babies do and all his major parts were normal. Father Bill came to the hospital and baptized him just in case. But Mike did fine; he was just very small. My mother always said he could fit in a shoebox. It was very hard for me to leave him in the hospital, but when it was time for me to go home, he had to stay for three more weeks. I had yet to hold him. As soon as he gained a little weight, I was allowed feed him once a day. So I drove the fifteen miles into the city to be with my son and hold him even though new mothers weren't to drive so soon after giving birth. When he weighed five pounds we were finally able to bring him home.

Mike slept in my old bassinet downstairs in the living room during the day so I wouldn't have to go up and down stairs several times a day. Kismet just could not understand who this little creature was that showed up in our house and was a threat to her. She would stand on a table by his bed and put her paws on the edge of the bassinet and just stare and sniff at him. She had never learned to get along with Dan, but a baby was different. She would lie in Mike's stroller when he wasn't in it and sit on the arm of my chair watching him while I fed him his bottle. At our home in Zanesville, I allowed Kismet outside for the first time in her life. She would stay close and watch Mike when we were outdoors.

When it came time to think about going back to school that August, I just could not bare to leave our child with strangers. Family was too far away. I would have to leave him with someone in Zanesville, but I didn't know anyone well. We decided I would quit teaching and stay home with Mike. I was not prepared for the joy of raising a child. Just to sit and watch him experience a mud puddle and a stick for the first time was a shock to me. Everything was brand new to him and such a delight to watch him discover the world. My mother thought Mike was perfect. She loved to take him for a day to the Fort Wayne Children's Zoo or to feed the ducks near where she lived.

I miscarried again and didn't get pregnant right away, like before. But I did eventually become pregnant and proved Mother wrong. It was possible for me to have children naturally. Mother was hoping I would have a girl. By now Burnie and Sandy had a son, Adam, and Zandra had a son, Clark, so Mother put in an order for a granddaughter. She was so sure this baby would also be born early like Mike was; she booked a group tour to Europe for just about the time our baby was due. Bob, Mother's husband, was gone by now for good and Mother was creating a new life for herself. In fact, Mother was in France for Bastille Day, July 14, 1974 when Carrie was born.

The week before Carrie's birth, Dan was in an industrial accident in the steel mill and his jaw was broken in two places. It was necessary for him to be transported to the hospital in order to wire his jaws shut. Since it was so very hot that July, and because Dan's face was swollen, to say nothing of the fact he was in pain, we moved into Mom's air-conditioned apartment. Burnie and his family were there also, so someone could take me to the hospital and care for Mike if necessary. During the first night the phone rang and it was Mother calling from France. She had called both our homes and after finding no one there, she tried her own number and found us all. I had to explain to her about Dan and why we were all in her apartment. She was upset about Dan's injuries with me being nine months pregnant, but she was too far away and couldn't do anything about it.

We stayed only a couple of days in the apartment until the swelling went down in Dan's jaw. The night we went home my labor began. I was determined to have Carrie naturally and did. With Mike I had had a spinal block. Carrie was born at nine o'clock on Sunday morning after a completely natural birth. During labor my blood pressure was high and didn't go down even after the birth. Doctors wanted to keep me in the hospital for several days to see why my blood pressure was so high. But I went home after the normal four days in the hospital and my blood pressure controlled itself in a few days.

Carrie was not the easy baby her brother had been. I nursed her until she drank from a cup at about nine months. Most of the day she screamed, if she wasn't nursing. But sitting in Grandpa Gump's old rocking chair and nursing her in the middle of the night was so calming to me after a hectic day. She didn't improve much with age and was a demanding child. Her shoes had to be tied just so and her pant's legs just the right length even at the age of three. And she still screamed when she didn't get her way. Dan and I would stand in the yard when she was screaming and jumping up and down so the neighbors could see we were not abusing her.

Carrie was fifteen months old when her sister Rachel was born in October of 1975. Rachel took forever to be born. I went almost three weeks over my due date. When the doctor said this had gone on long enough, I was ready. Mother came and took Mike and Carrie home with her in the afternoon. Dan took me to the hospital that evening and when the doctor broke my water it was near midnight. I had one or two strong pains and Rachel was crowning. Dan had attended the Red Cross classes so he could be with me when this new baby was born. He helped roll me into the delivery room and then everything stopped. Dr. Ram and the nurse stood there with their gloved hands in the air and I was waiting to push. The minutes ticked by. Finally, Rachel arrived on her own sweet time and she has not changed. She is still late.

That first day I was home from the hospital, some nasty neighbor kids killed Kismet. I was devastated. She had been my companion for twelve years. Never before in my life had I been allowed to have a pet longer than a few weeks. Dan buried her under our beautiful flowering crab tree. I had three children including a brand new baby and life continued.

By the time Rachel was born, Burnie was doing home repairs and home construction work. He asked Mother and she agreed to let him build her a new home. She bought a lovely wooded corner lot with many old trees. Several trees were hickory trees with nuts for her to use. Burnie built her a beautiful home. Over the years, he remodeled it until at last she did have her perfect house. She planned to die there.

Mother now had three granddaughters and seven grandsons. Zandra and Bruce had two sons, Clark and Tyler. After twenty-three years of marriage, the doctor's son proved not to be the husband Mother always thought he was. Bruce and Zandra divorced. Burnie and Sandy also had two sons, Adam and Leith. Sandy and Burnie's marriage ended far sooner than twenty-three years. Years later Burnie married Rhonda and they had a son, Brad and a daughter, Alex. Burnie adopted Aaron, Rhonda's son from a previous marriage.

Every summer after Rachel was born we went to Colorado. In the mid 1970's, Dan bought some land just west of Divide, Colorado, thirty-five miles west of Colorado Springs. He bought it without conferring with me first. Dan was so excited he had to show everyone his piece of the mountains. We all piled into the car and drove to Sherwood Forest to see this piece of land. Rachel was not yet old enough to walk. Everyone else got out and walked all over the hill covered with forest at the end of Jolly Rogue Drive. I stayed in the car with Rachel completely forgotten. I could not walk over uneven ground and carry a baby. This reminded me of something my Father would do. Although I liked to travel and enjoyed the scenery, I was never happy or comfortable at the cabin Dan built and I named Bear Paw. The name came from bear tracks found in the freshly-graded driveway.

The "A" frame cabin was complete but unfinished inside. We spent many summers at Bear Paw as a family in this stationary teepee. To this day, we do not have electricity or a well for water. At first we had nothing and it was educational for the kids to learn to entertain themselves without neighbor friends or bikes or TV. Dan worked hard at getting the cabin as livable as possible, with a generator and large buried water tank; we eventually had some comforts. Every evening Dan fell asleep on the couch after the kids were in bed and I sat there cold, alone with a sleeping man and bugs and mice and tried to read by lantern light and feed wood into the wood stove for a little heat. Every day of this so-called vacation, I had to do everything I did at home only under primitive conditions. We did have a propane gas cook stove but had to use a bucket of water to flush the toilet. And we had to heat great quantities of water on the stove for baths and hair washings. Bear Paw is at 9300 feet altitude and it can get very chilly even in July. It rained most afternoons often with hail that piled up next to the cabin. This was not my idea of a vacation, year after year. As the kids grew older and no one was in diapers and they could dress themselves, it became a little better. I bought books about Colorado wild flowers and learned the different kinds of trees and birds. I enjoyed traveling around the state but I was out of my element and try as I would, I never felt comfortable at Bear Paw. I wanted broad-leafed trees. However, the cabin was, and is, Dan's pride and joy.

Chapter 31

$\mathcal{B}$ack home in Indiana, I was becoming my mother in many ways. I began making all the bread we ate. I canned tomatoes and tomato juice from Dan's garden. I would buy baskets of peaches, corn, pears and apples. I froze the corn, peaches and beans and made applesauce to freeze. We picked blueberries and strawberries to freeze or make into jellies and jams. Dan only liked French salad dressing so I learned how to make it and make it the right color so he thought it was the store bought brand. I also made most of the kids clothes, something Mother never did. Having three small children meant I needed to do the laundry every day, and even though we had a dryer, I enjoyed hanging the wash outside for the sun to dry in nice weather. That meant I had to carry baskets of wet wash up the basement steps and outside. Dan would help with the carrying if he was home. When dry, I had to take the clothes off the line and carry them inside, fold them and carry them upstairs to be put away. My children soon learned to carry their own clothes up those same stairs my Mother worried about. And by the time they each reached age ten, they were doing their own laundry, including their bedding.

As the children grew older, they had to help me more and more around the house. During the oil crises in the 70's, we had a wood stove installed in the living room and a smaller one placed in the upstairs den. Dan bought a cord of wood and stacked it in the yard. Our three children carried loads of wood into the garage, out of the weather, every week. But daily, they had to carry baskets of wood up stairs from the garage and then some of it had to go on upstairs to the den for use in the two wood stoves. There was no way I could have managed that job daily on my own.

In addition, they carried untold numbers of buckets of canned vegetables to the fruit cellar for me, as well as freezer boxes of food to be stored in the garage freezer. They each received a small allowance and could spend it on anything they fancied. Usually they spent it on candy at the neighborhood store where one or the other of them was often sent to pick up milk or some other much needed item. I could not get up the high step without a banister into the store. The day came when I could no longer walk the block to the post office to pick up the mail, so they were sent to do that job for me. Before that, I spent many years walking a mile around town several times a week. I did this to help with weight control and I enjoyed the walks around Zanesville. Carrie and Rachel often tagged along with me. When they were old enough, Dan divided the yard into thirds and each child could mow the grass in their third for five dollars. If Rachel was babysitting or if Carrie or Mike were otherwise not home, whoever was home could mow any one else's third and receive the extra five dollars. This arrangement worked well until they went off to college or full time employment.

I tried so hard to prove to myself that I could be just as good a mother as my mother and grandmothers had been. But underlying this was the fact that I was also proving to myself that I was an able-bodied woman living a normal life. Close friends and relatives always forgot I was handicapped until I came up against some obstacle I simply could not conquer and needed help. Asking for help was not in my vocabulary. It was easier to have one of my children do it for me.

Soon after Mike was born, we started attending St. Aloysius Catholic Church. Our priest called and asked me to teach first and second combined grades at St. Aloysius School in 1981. I knew he was a very intense man and I wasn't sure I wanted to work for him. After talking it over with Dan, I agreed to teach. Mike was taken out of Ossian Public School and enrolled at St. Al's. Carrie was in the first grade. I would be her teacher for two years. God was telling me I would learn to get along with this difficult child. We did fine and even became friends. Rachel was in kindergarten and stayed with a family friend in the afternoons. The second year I had both of my daughters in my classroom.

Those two years of teaching at St. Aloysius were both rewarding and stressful. Father was not only our parish priest, he was principal of the school and he ran the school in a very old fashioned closed atmosphere. Parents never visited classrooms. Teachers were not allowed to take sick leave or personal days. If it was absolutely unavoidable, Father was the substitute teacher. Each teacher did her own recess duty. Even at lunch we had to eat with the students and then take turns going outside for duty every day. There was never teacher planning time during the day. The school was locked and we could not even come and work on Saturday. Dan came twice a week and picked up our children after school and I stayed until five o'clock to get my planning done for the next few days. The only outside person allowed into the school was the male public school speech teacher.

When I had a student I thought had learning problems, I asked Father if I could have him tested by a professional. Father told me just to try harder to teach that child. I did have one child tested by the speech teacher, unknown to Father. We found the child had suffered a severe hearing loss in early childhood and was therefore behind his age group in learning to read. Even with these kinds of stressful unprofessional occurrences, I found much personal satisfaction being back in the classroom and teaching young children. I was learning things I had not learned in public school or in college. The Catholic schools taught an excellent phonics-based reading program which made reading easy to teach and learn. And of course, I was learning more about the church I had chosen by being involved in daily prayers and several masses during the week. There were only one hundred students, grades one through eight, in this four- room school. All rooms had double grades and each teacher taught her own art, music and physical education. Father taught religion to each grade and those were just about the only times he was in the school. Yet every child did well academically. But under the surface, everyone was always fearful Father would spank them with his paddle or make them kneel in church for an extended period. To make sure test scores were high, students were given personal attention with tutoring whenever possible before or after school. He had to approve all report cards before they were given to the parents. With all of the outward appearances of a successful school, Father took all the credit and the teachers were just a small part of his school. It became so frustrating dealing with a man who was more interested in the appearance of the school than in the best interest of the children and faculty. I decided I could not continue teaching at St. Aloysius.

Our children were switched back into the public school in the village of Ossian. I substituted in that school for two years, but it was not nearly as satisfying as having my own classroom. However, I was able to know my children's teachers and friends well. Ossian School had three floors and on more than a few days I had trouble climbing those three flights of steps that seemed to increase each time.

In 1985 I was asked to return to teaching at St. Aloysius. We now had a new priest, Father Hodde. He was kind and gentle and cared a great deal about the students and staff but he was the parish priest and not the school principal. The school now had a real principal. Again I taught first and second grades. Carrie and Rachel returned to Catholic school with me. Mike was in a public middle school by this time and he wanted to stay. Dan and I agreed he could stay. Mary Schreiber was our new principal and the doors were opened for real learning to occur without fear. Two years later, I became principal of the school and expanded what Mary had started. I updated the school even more with hot lunches, art and music teachers, computers and special education consultants when needed.

When Rachel was eleven, she became very ill with tonsillitis and never seemed to get completely over it. One day after school, the girls were waiting for me to finish up my work so we could go home. Rachel said she was so tired she didn't think she could climb the stairs. That scared me and I took her to the doctor again. He ran several tests and found she was diabetic. She, along with the rest of us in the family, spent a week in the hospital learning to live with this disease. We all learned to give shots by practicing on an orange and also learned to test blood sugar levels. Rachel quickly learned to give her own shots. Planning her meals and testing her blood often took time and practice. She adjusted very well. Carrie was always concerned about her sister and watched and learned all she could. Mike, being a boy, was more interested in baseball. A couple of years later, we sent Rachel to diabetic summer camp. What a surprise to find it was at Camp Mack, the church camp of my youth. I walked around looking for familiar places. The vespers campfire, Jacob's Well and the church were all there only smaller than in my memory. I made the mistake of looking into the church to see and smell all those beautiful, aromatic wood shaving curls on the floor and I found they had been replaced with rocks. Rachel had the time of her life and I had walked back into my past.

During these years, Mother continued to teach. She moved to a newer school closer to her home. To fill the lonely hours after school, she did volunteer work, joined several women's groups and taught home-bound children after school. She and Bob were long over and she had taken back the name Gump. Men were still a problem for her. That old ingrained idea that a woman needed a man plagued her and she was always looking for that companion for her old age. She dated Phil for over fourteen years. He even gave her a diamond ring, but she would not marry him. He was in the Shriners and took her to all their social events, which she enjoyed. Phil was a nice man but just not the man Mother wanted to marry.

Mother reluctantly retired in 1983 from teaching. The school had a big party for her and then she went home and was alone, but not for long. Years before she retired, she had started volunteering at Parkview Hospital. She sat at the front desk for years and really enjoyed meeting doctors and scores of people needing help. After she retired, she volunteered in the gift shop and this was pure joy for her. She was able to see all the marvelous items that came into the shop before they were even priced. Vera Bradley bags, jewelry, and trinkets for her grandchildren were special delights. Mother made many close friends with the other volunteer ladies. My mother had three hobbies she dearly loved. Cooking, growing flowers and shopping for gifts for her family. Now she worked in a gift shop and received a discount! We all benefited from her volunteer job. She joined the Fort Wayne Woman's Club and a lady's investment group. Her calendar was full of lunch dates and evening gatherings. And of course, she made sure that all the holiday dinners were at her house for the family.

By the late 1980's I was noticing physical changes in myself. I was becoming so tired I would come home from school and fall asleep sitting in a chair. I couldn't walk as far as I once did. Standing on chairs to put things up on the bulletin board was impossible. Carrie and Rachel had to do it for me. I was slowing down big time and I blamed this fatigue on gaining weight at mid-life and aging. This physical slowing down played an important part in my decision to become principal and leave the classroom. I thought the office would be less physical work than the classroom. It was true up to a point but being a principal was so much more draining mentally. The many meetings meant putting in much longer hours and often traveling to cities fifty miles away for retreats and conferences for Catholic school principals, to say nothing of the emotional drain when trying to keep peace between children, parents, teachers, a priest and the State of Indiana. Being the principal of a small school is often more draining and harder work than having the same position in a large school where there are assistant administrators and several secretaries. In my case, I taught some classes, did recess duty, lunchroom duty and the Christmas program along with all the duties of being an administrator.

Seven of the nine years I was a principal, Dan worked second shift at Slater Steel and we didn't see each other during the week. He came to church and went to mass with me every Friday morning and we talked on the phone daily and still shared the same bed. Our marriage was strong but the burden of raising the children fell mainly to me because he was gone in the evenings. I went to volleyball games, football games, basketball games, and all the practices, as well as parent teacher conferences and high school back to school night. I found I was just wearing out. Then I began to hear about Post Polio Syndrome, where people who had had polio forty to fifty years earlier were now showing polio symptoms again. Of course, didn't think that applied to me. I thought I had gained back some weight, was getting a little older and that was slowing me down.

I heard of a Post Polio or PPS group meeting in a nearby branch of the Allen County Library and I went just out of curiosity. The room was packed and people started telling their stories and I soon learned that I probably did have PPS. I had some aches and pains and I was often exhausted at the end of the day. My hands and feet were always freezing to the point where our school custodian placed a small electric heater under my desk. I tried to tell myself it would not get any worse and I could live with this. My children were growing up and sometimes I was actually home alone with no one to help carry things upstairs or the groceries up the basement steps into the kitchen from the garage. I was paying Carrie to clean the house. I just had no extra energy. Dan even bought me a fold up cane I could use if necessary. I applied for and received a handicapped parking permit for the car, but was reluctant to use it.

In the fall of 1993, I finally went to the only doctor with a Post Polio Syndrome clinic in Ft. Wayne. Dr. Steven Cremer had a rehabilitation clinic. They worked with people with many handicaps at this clinic, especially industrial accidents, but he was the one doctor in Fort Wayne who knew about PPS. Polio was perceived to be a long dead disease and most doctors had never seen a case of polio let alone a case of obscure post polio. I went through this clinic, seeing a physical as well as an occupational therapist. After a battery of several different kinds of tests, Dr. Cremer told me I did have Post Polio Syndrome. My first question was how long would I be able to continue to work? He told me I would be lucky to be able to work three more years. He also told me I should remove as much stress from my life as possible and rest often. Those were the only things I could do to slow the progress of my condition. This was another life changing event for me. I didn't want to stop working. But I did know that if I continued in my high stress job, I would lose my independent mobility sooner rather than later.

So I started putting my ducks in a row. I informed Father Hodde I would be working only a couple more years. I explained Post Polio Syndrome to Dan and our children and told them what was happening to me. They all nodded their heads and went on with their lives. They lived with me and didn't notice the gradual changes. It is very difficult to accept that your wife or mother was very slowly becoming an invalid. I understood this, but it was not very comforting to me.

Mother understood immediately. She was slowing down herself but from age. In many ways we were becoming similar with our physical problems. She had lived through my childhood illness and recovery and knew just how devastating polio was. Now I was looking at some of the same problems reoccurring without the hope of recovery. As Mother aged, she mellowed much as her mother had. She became less judgmental and more accepting of other points of view. As a consequence, we became better friends. She depended on me more and I on her.

Chapter 32

On the fall of 1994, I accidentally found out Rachel was pregnant. She was nineteen, in college and unmarried. I waited until we were alone in the house and then I asked her about it. She admitted it was true. I tried to not place blame but to let her know we would help with what ever she decided to do. But the decision was hers; we would not make the decision for her. She told me she and Andy, her boyfriend, were going to give the baby up for adoption because they felt they were too immature to raise a child and they were not ready to get married. It was a rough winter.

I was now using a cane when grocery shopping and spent as much time as possible sitting at school. I dropped out of most of the diocesan committees I was on and generally tried to simplify my life. I was also planting the seed that we needed to move to a one-story house. Now I had Dan's attention. He doesn't like change and most certainly didn't want to move to a different house.

Alicia Rose, our first grandchild, was born in April 1995. Rachel, being a diabetic, had a rough time and Alicia was born cesarean. Andy's family would not let him sign the adoption papers. Rachel would not allow her child to be fought over, so Alicia came to live with us as a much loved and desired little girl. Friends from school went garage sale shopping for baby furniture for us and in no time we were ready and most happy to have Alicia join us. Mike was employed and no longer lived with us, but Carrie was still living at home and going to school in Fort Wayne. Between us all, Rachel had help. But it was made clear, Alicia was her baby and she was responsible for her.

Our home was put up for sale. It sold sooner than we expected. After being unable to find a house we liked, we bought a vacant lot in Zanesville two blocks from our old home. Mother had a friend with a manufactured home and I really liked the open floor plan, always keeping in the back of my mind the day would come when I would be in a wheelchair. Dan and I picked out the house we wanted and had it placed on our lot in the early fall of 1995. I was working my last year at school. I would be fifty-five in late September and therefore was entitled to a small retirement from the Catholic schools.

Zanesville was putting in a sewer system and because of all the problems with that project we could not live in our new house for months. We moved into a neighbor's house while they wintered in Texas. Carrie, Rachel, Alicia, Dan and I were living in close quarters. That winter, Mother was hospitalized because of back pain. I took a day off from school and spent it with her. After several tests the doctor told me Mother had the spine of a young woman and never let anyone operate on her back. She went home the next day and complained of back pain off and on until her death.

In April 1996, the sewer system was still not completed in Zanesville, but we had to move. This time a lady in town told us we could rent her mother's farmhouse at the edge of Zanesville. Her mother was very elderly and had moved in with her. The house was furnished and we moved in and tried to make do. Carrie was now engaged to Mike Savarese. Our Mike was dating Kim and Rachel and Andy were seeing each other again. We lived on the farm for four long months. Finally the Zanesville town council and the sewer company engineers said we could move into our new home on August 1. Dan, Carrie and I cheated and slept in our new home July 31.

The entire ordeal had taken a bigger toll on Dan than on anyone else. He did understand I needed to be out of a three-story house. I had lived in that house for twenty-five years. Me, the kid who moved every year had actually lived in the same house for twenty-five years. It was extremely difficult for me to move also, but I had no choice. If I wanted to keep my independence, I had to reduce my physical activity.

I retired from St. Aloysius in June of 1996 after 14 years of rewarding experiences. It was sad to leave but it was still our parish and I continued to be on parish committees. I was able to see the students in church and see how tall they grew and listen to their life adventures when they chose to share them with me.

Carrie graduated from Purdue University and soon after married Mike Savarese. Rachel and Andy married a year later when their daughter Alicia was three. Mike and Kim married the same year at Bear Paw in Colorado. Kim had two children from a previous marriage so we had two step grandchildren. Our children were gone just as fast as they came and all of a sudden Dan and I were alone. He was very happy to have me home. We settled into our new life easily. More grandchildren began arriving with Carrie giving birth to Jasmine. Carrie and Rachel were both working in mental health. Rachel had settled into nurses training after trying several fields of endeavor. Mike was entering a new field in tool and die working with a laser jet. In September 2001, Carrie had her second daughter, Lauren. Life was good.

And I finally got a dog. A fellow teacher gave Frampe to me. His mother was a miniature poodle and his father was unknown. When Mother was retiring she wanted a pet so I agreed to take Frampe and train him until Mother was ready to keep him. But Mother wasn't home enough for a dog and we had all grown attached to him, so he became a permanent family member. Frampe came up missing in August of 1999. We never found a trace of him. He was old and had some health problems but still had a zest for life. I think I miss him more than I missed Kismet since I had no babies to take his place. We just had grouchy Pookie, the cat.

Mother's life was running its course. She now had great grandchildren to shop and cook for. The entire family gathered at her house for big holidays and seasonal birthday parties. Burnie began taking care of her yard and snow removal. In the spring she still insisted on planting flower boxes and beds and hanging many flower baskets. Burnie and his kids helped her. She simply loved her home and still entertained often. She held the White Cross Volunteers Garage Sale from Parkview Hospital at her house every year. Plus she had a pot of chili on the stove and a dessert waiting for the workers. Her hair was styled in a very sophisticated manner every week. Her nails were done every couple of weeks with false tips. She cared how she appeared and never looked frumpy.

CNN was her mainstay and then she decided FOX news was better. She read the daily newspaper cover to cover. Her appointment calendar was full to overflowing with brunches and lunches. She had friends by the dozens and still was able to drive her car. She did concede to buying strawberries, blueberries and corn already picked, but she still froze food like there would be a great natural disaster tomorrow. And she still was drying corn, which was an all day job. I had always disliked that job. First the corn had to be husked, and then the silk brushed off and then all the corn cut off the cob of twenty-four ears of corn. And corn only grows and ripens in the hottest time of summer so the corn silk stuck to your damp skin, to say nothing of having to cook and stir it all day. It was a nasty job. As the years progressed, this became another job for Burnie, Brad and Alex. Mother did the cooking part all day but they helped her with the husking. She gave Burnie her corn drier when the day came she felt she could no longer use it.

For family meals she fixed specific special foods for each person. For Dan she made deviled eggs and dried corn. Blueberry muffins were made for Burnie and his kids. Baked beans always for Burnie. She made homemade ice cream for all, pumpkin pie for Mike, black olives for Carrie, Rachel and then Alicia. Rolls for everyone, but she made sure there were enough for Andy and Mike to take some home. Her life now revolved around her family and special friends. She was no longer trying to find a husband. She finally broke off her relationship with Phil because she knew she would never marry again. However, when Phil was dying in the VA hospital, she went to see him twice every week.

After I retired I spent more time with Mother. We became friends again and often talked about times only we remembered. I took her to her doctor appointments because she had so many questions and didn't listen to the answers. She was always changing doctors for this problem or that ache. She said two pairs of ears were better than one pair. Her health began to deteriorate. She had congestive heart failure; kidney problems as well as long time high blood pressure. She was taking multitudes of pills and was in fear of confusing them. Rachel got her a medicine box and showed her how to fill it. Diabetes became a problem with more pills at different times of the day and blood monitoring, and again Rachel was there to help.

Mother developed double vision years ago and had prisms put in her glasses. We all worried about her driving. Now that I was not working, I drove her to Pekin, Illinois to visit Zandra. I also drove her to the doctor's office for appointments. At one time she had four different regular doctors. She had trouble keeping it all straight and wrote notes to herself and lists of questions to ask the doctor. She never wanted to throw out pills left over when her prescription was changed. I would go through it all with her and check all the lists from all the doctors. Then I would throw out the pills no longer needed. Next time, I would find the old pills back in her closet, some of them years old and from doctors she couldn't even remember.

Very slowly she was losing control of her life and she was well aware of it. Even so, she still fought for what control she could keep. Burnie now drove her to Turkey Run State Park for the family outing every Thanksgiving. But she would cook a turkey dinner for some of us the week before anyway. Burnie started balancing her checkbook. Little by little her life was becoming narrow. It was a big step when she hired a cleaning lady and let her wash the windows. Mother was so afraid the neighbors would think she was lazy! So much like her mother had been. And she worried about spending the money she wanted to leave for her children. She started to spend more time visiting with us. After a meal she didn't hop up and clean the table and start the dishwashing right away. She wanted to sit and said the dishes weren't going anywhere. Just the opposite of what she taught me. If there was a big family gathering, she now sat and let Rhonda, Zandra and others clean up afterwards. It was sad to see her just sit and she hated it.

One year for Christmas, Rhonda had written to all Mother's friends in Goshen and Fort Wayne and had them send a letter about Mom and memories they shared. Rhonda put all the letters in a book for Mom. It was such a nice gift and Mother was so pleased. Another Christmas, Rhonda and Burnie bought Mother a white flocked tree with clusters of red balls and spotlights; what a joy for Mom.

The year Mother turned eighty-three Zandra planted eighty-three white petunias in Mother's yard. In 1999 I bought her a white phalaenopsis orchid plant that was blooming. She placed it in her west facing bay window and nursed it. It grew several new sprouts, but never bloomed again after that spring.

For Mother's eighty-fifth birthday, Rhonda and Burnie arranged a lawn party and invited as many of Mother's friends as possible. Burnie had landscaped his back yard into a lovely city garden room with a gold fish pool and an arbor for trumpet vines. All the grandchildren pitched in and paid for a limousine to pick up Mother and a few close friends and bring them to the party. It was a great day for her.

Mom was slowing down a good deal but still able to care for herself. She had been talking about dying and told me I wasn't taking her seriously. She thought she just would die in her sleep and we would find her body and be devastated. For years she had been giving away little mementoes to family members. Grandkids were asked what they wanted of her things so she could make of record of their desires and see they got it after her death. As far back as in the 80's she was preparing us. So many times she said, "Next year for Christmas I probably won't be here," that we began to ignore it.

Chapter 33

In 2000, Zandra turned fifty and I turned sixty. Zan was working on her master's degree from the University of Illinois and was also dating a man she knew from high school, Tim Bower. Mother kept saying that if she knew Zandra had a good man to take care of her, she could die in peace. Of course, Zandra by now knew she didn't need a man. She would marry only when and if she really wanted to.

The following March, Dan and I went on our annual trip to Clearwater, Florida for a week with Dan's mom, Betsy and Father Bill. Dan had a very bad case of bronchitis and we left a day later than normal so he could rest in bed. But he was pretty sick most of the vacation. By Wednesday of that week, I had his bronchitis. We arrived home on Sunday and Tuesday I was hospitalized with double pneumonia. Mother called me every day, but she could not drive to visit me. I went home on Saturday not feeling really great so I didn't go see Mom and expose her to my illness. Monday I was back in the hospital and couldn't breathe. I had a bad asthma attack, but I didn't have asthma! I spent another seven days in the hospital until they had it figured out. The blood pressure beta blocker pills I had been on for fifteen years should not have been taken by anyone with weakened muscles. The medication was changed and I very slowly recovered. I have been on oxygen at night ever since.

Mother was so upset when Dan told her about my illness and that he had called our priest he was so worried about me. Mother had Burnie's sixteen-year-old Brad drive her to Bluffton on a snowy Sunday just to make sure I was going to live. It was hard for her to walk any distance but she was determined to see me.

Later that spring, Mother began having serious problems. She was falling and probably more often than she told us. She fell outside her front door in the evening while watering her hanging baskets. She couldn't get up and lay there at least an hour before Rae next door heard her and got her up and inside. Her arm was broken. After she fell again a few days later, Burnie had her admitted to Parkview Hospital. Because of her congestive heart and kidney problems, it took a month to get her body fluids regulated. They told her she could no longer live alone. That broke her heart. We had a family meeting in the hospital to help her decide what she wanted to do, move to assisted living or have around the clock home care. Of course, she wanted neither. But finally she agreed to let us look for an assisted living apartment. Zandra and I spent two days visiting places Mother recommended. We narrowed it down to two possible facilities. We took Mom out of the hospital in a wheel chair for several hours to visit these places. She chose a lovely apartment at Heritage Park, less than a mile from her home. We also took her back to her house and we three had lunch together in the home her son built for her that she loved so much.

Mom moved into her new apartment on July 3, 2001. She now had to use a walker although she tried not to. At first she didn't want to go to the dining room at Heritage Park because all the ladies had white hair.

Zandra finished her Master's degree the end of July. She decided to move with Tim to South Bend at the end of August. Mother was thrilled. Zandra would only be two hours away instead of five and Mother liked Tim and his family very much. Dan and Tim had worked together at Slater Steels at one time and Tim's parents and siblings still lived in Fort Wayne. Everything seemed to be falling into place for Zandra. Mother said many times that, "If Tim will marry Zandra, I could die in peace."

Zandra and Tim moved into the renovated Central High School Apartments in South Bend in August. Their apartment had been the high school's pool. Mother just couldn't get over that they lived in a pool. On August 22, Tim and Zandra eloped. Mother was happy and disappointed. She wanted them to get married in her church so she could invite all her friends and have a party. Mother was happy Tim and Zan were married, but she just had to see that pool apartment. So on August 24, Dan and I picked up Mother and drove her to South Bend. It was a very long day for her but she was happy to see where her daughter was living and that there was no water in the pool, only carpet and living room furniture. After going out for dinner, we took Mom home. Dan commented to me that he hadn't realized she had such difficulty breathing. And it was true; Mother was finding it harder and harder to breathe.

In October, I had her admitted to the hospital again for a few days to get her breathing under control. And then in November she was back in the hospital because everything was again out of balance and she was losing it mentally. We thought she would die at that time. Burnie or I sat with her. Zandra and Tim came and sat with her. After a month in the hospital, she finally came around mentally.

Mother spent Christmas at my house. Father Bill and Betsy were the only other people there for dinner. It was a nice quiet sunny day. In the evening, all our children and their children stopped in. Zandra and her family also came by. This time it was Mother's last Christmas and I think we all knew it. Mother had a happy day with her family.

By Easter, Mother was visibly declining. She was having trouble standing and walking. Early in April, Mother and I visited the kidney dialysis center at Lutheran Hospital at her doctor's request. We watched a video on how dialysis works and then the social worker came in and talked to us. She asked if we wanted to see the room where dialysis was performed. Mother said no, but I said I would like to see it. When I returned to the room, Mother was crying. She said she did not want dialysis and didn't want to talk about it anymore. She signed papers stating she was informed, but declined dialysis and then we left. By the end of April, she was really bad. She was falling again and Heritage Park was calling Burnie in the middle of the night to help pick her up. On April 18, Burnie, Mother and I met with her kidney doctor. He told us her kidneys were getting worse and she should think about Hospice because they were so good with pain control.

Mom called Parkview Hospice. Marsha, a hospice nurse, came and talked to Mother and me on Friday April 26th. She told Mother to decide what she wanted to happen when she could no longer care for herself. Mother had planned everything for the end of her life so carefully and completely, but she had never considered she would reach a point where she could not care for herself. On Sunday April 28, we had another family meeting to decide what to do. Mother could not make that decision, or would not. She did not want to live with one of us. She would consider the nursing home or home care. She had always told me nursing homes were dead ends and I knew she didn't want that. Rachel said there was no question; Mother should die in her own apartment with her familiar belongings near her. I talked to Mom and it was agreed we would get home care. The next Thursday, the hospice doctor and Marsha came to Mom's and talked to us. They went over her medicines and decided on a plan of action. They would not try to prolong her life and they would not hasten the end of her life. But they would make her comfortable and let her die naturally.

The next day, Mom fell again. She was put to bed with a catheter and never again walked. She was losing touch with reality again. We took turns staying with her. Burnie spent the night there on May 5 to make sure she stayed in bed. The next morning he called Doris, a home care person to come and care for Mother. I was there at 9:30 that morning and Doris was in charge. She worked seven to seven every day during the week caring for Mom. Linda came at seven in the evening and worked until seven in the morning so Mother had around the clock care.

For awhile Mother did very well. Doris took her for walks outside in her wheel chair and she had more visitors than was good for her. Hospice was wonderful. They provided a hospital bed, bedside commode, bed table; wheel chair, oxygen and a lovely lady came three times a week to bathe Mother.

Zandra and Tim visited Mother the weekend before her 87th birthday. They decorated her apartment with balloons and streamers and Zandra painted Mother's toenails each a different color. On Mother's June 4th birthday, I made her a fresh strawberry pie. Burnie bought a pizza and we sent Doris home so we could eat supper with Mom alone. Heritage Park had cake and ice cream for her in the dining room at noon and Doris and I had taken her down in a wheel chair so she could enjoy the celebration with her friends.

I went to see her every other day at least. We had some long talks about dying. I told her about my college friend Bill, the guy who took me for a convertible ride in a snowstorm. Bill and two of his college friends had always thought they would die young and they did. These three guys had all agreed on an outlandish thing they would make happen after they died to prove there was an after life, all the roots of the trees in their backyards would face the sky. I don't know what happened when Bob and Rick died, but Peggy, his sister, told me about Bill. He had cancer and died when he was in his fifties, the last of the three college friends. Two weeks after he died a tornado went through his town. It didn't touch his house but uprooted all the trees in his backyard.

And I told Mother about Dan's cousin. One year when we were in Colorado, Rick was killed by a landslide. We were there for the wake and funeral and all the family mourning. Back home in Indiana we had a six-year-old peony bush that had never bloomed. That next spring, as I was working in the garden, I told Rick to see if he could make that peony bloom. And in a few weeks it did. Mother turned her head, looked at me and said, "So what do you want me to make bloom?" I was so surprised I couldn't think of anything. Finally, I told her to make something bloom that wasn't supposed to be there. I remembered the white orchid I had given her. She had told me to take it when we cleaned out her house. So I told her to make the orchid bloom.

The spring was cold and wet. Carrie didn't get my shockingly pink

wave petunias planted along the driveway until late in May. I had bought
bigger plants because of the late season. With the progression of Post Polio,
I now had an electric power wheelchair I used when outside or when going
any distance like in the mall or at the zoo. In my power chair I could help
Carrie with the planting of my petunias and I could care for them.

In April, I told Mother that Rachel was expecting a baby. Her first
reaction was that one generation leaves and another one comes. She loved
Carrie's Lauren and held her as much as she could. She told Jasmine and
Alicia to take things they wanted from her trinket shelves. Carrie went to
see Mom every week. Our son Mike was with Mother when her motorized
water mattress came from Hospice. He showed her all the things it could
do; waves or bubbles fast or slow. They had a good time with it. All the
grandchildren came to see her. Everyone knew the end was near.

On Thursday evening, June 27, I called Mom. She talked to me,
but she was hard to understand. There was a gurgle in her throat. I told her
I would be to see her in the morning. She told me to sleep in and not to get
there too early. I was there about 10:30 on Friday morning. She was awake
and alert. We talked about the terrible rainstorm that hit Fort Wayne on
Tuesday. Her right arm was hurting her and she had trouble moving it. If I
moved it for her she could scratch her nose. Louise, the new lady, was on
for weekend duty and gave Mom a dose of morphine for the pain. I stayed
with Mother about three hours. She was sleeping when I left.

On Saturday I didn't go to see her until the afternoon. But I called
the first thing every morning to see how her night had been. That morning
she had eaten oatmeal and then went back to sleep. I went in after lunch
and sat beside her bed. She was awake and was staring at the ceiling and
her mouth was moving without any sound coming out. Her arms were at
her side. Her hands with the painted pearl pink acrylic nails never moved.
I talked to her but she never responded. About an hour later, Carrie and her
family came. I went out in the living room and told Carrie not to be surprised but Mom would not know her or respond to her. But when they

walked in Mom did know them. Carrie hugged her and told her she loved her and Mom said she loved her too. Mother said hi to everyone and told Carrie to take good care of her family. I walked Carrie and her family to the door when they left. When I went back and sat down beside Mom, she looked at me and said, "You're still here!" Those were the last words Mother said to me.

Early Monday morning, July 1, I called Marsha and asked her to meet us at Mom's and tell us exactly what was happening. Burnie and I got there at 10:30. Zandra had been there a while. Doris was working. We all met in Mother's room and Marsha asked me to take Mother's temperature under her arm. I did. She had a high fever and her kidneys were not working and her heart was very weak. Marsha told us Mother would be gone today or tomorrow. When Marsha left, she kissed Mother's forehead and told her she would see her again some day. Burnie had apartment buildings with flooded basements he had to see to so he left to get his work organized. Zandra and I sat and listened to Mother struggle to breathe, and to the gurgling in her throat. Time seemed to stand still between her breaths. We found a clock with a second hand and timed the seconds between her breaths. We kept thinking any minute she would just stop breathing and it would be all over.

Finally I asked Doris," How do you know when someone is dead besides when the breathing stops?" She would not talk in the room with Mother, so we went into the living room. Doris told us people die feet first. Their feet get cold and it moves up their bodies. All the phlegm in Mother's throat would come out and her eyes would open. She said we would not want to be in the room when it happened, but right now she still had a high temperature and it would still be awhile before she died.

Burnie came back and he sat with us. We all took turns telling Mom it was okay, she had done her best with her life and she had our permission to leave. There were some sticks with sponge on the ends to dip in water and moisten her lips. Burnie did that often and she would moan like it felt good. I had to get up and walk up and down the hall. I was full of nervous energy. Back in her room, I cleaned dresser drawers. She had given most of her clothes away, but the drawers still needed cleaning. We sat and waited. It was a very long day just sitting and listening to my mother's breath and waiting for it to stop. Linda came on duty at seven that evening. She told us after caring for dying people for over twenty years she had never had anyone die on her watch, and she didn't expect Mother to die that night. I left at 10:30 p.m.; I had to get some sleep. Burnie and Zandra stayed a little while longer.

The next morning I called and Zandra said Mom's feet were cold. So I drove the twenty-eight miles to Mother's apartment right away. Burnie had been there and left. I went to Mother and kissed her and told her it was time to go see Jesus and Grandma Gump. I could see the phlegm in her mouth. I sat down beside Zandra and told her Rachel had gone to the doctor about her baby the day before and I had never thought to call her. So I called her at work. As I was talking to Rachel, Doris came in and cleaned out Mother's mouth and Mom started coughing. I hung up quick and Zandra said, "Of all the books we have read, why anyone didn't write about dying as being like this?" She jumped up and left the room for a minute, standing in the doorway and then went for a towel Doris asked for. Doris stood in front of Mom so I could not see her face. Mother coughed again. She took one last deep breath and that was all. Doris said, "She is gone." She went to the phone to call hospice. Zandra said "That's unbelievable, you were talking to Rachel about the next generation just as Mother was leaving us." Doris grabbed Zandra and me and we all held hands over Mother's body and Doris led us in prayer. And then a hospice nurse was there and she and Doris wanted to prepare Mother's body. Zandra grabbed the tissue box and we went out and sat on Mother's patio bench and cried. The sky was so blue it broke my heart and a wren was singing in the trees and my Mother had just died.

Chapter 34

$\mathcal{O}$n July 5, Mother's memorial service was held just like she had planned. My father's two living sisters were there, Aunt Grace and Aunt Blanche, as well as several of Dad's cousins. Evelyn and Helen, two dearly loved Goshen friends came to say good bye. I was surprised at the number of people who attended because Mother was so elderly. I should have known better. She was a friend of so many people of different ages. Rachel, Carrie and Burnie gave wonderful eulogies. I'm sure Mother was pleased with the service and the reception. Her body, painted toenails included, was taken to Indianapolis to the medical school for use in teaching medical students. Some day her ashes will be returned to us and we will sprinkle them on the rose garden in Lakeside Park as she requested.

After the service, we ate dinner as Mom had planned for us at Nick's Rib Room. There was little sadness present. Mother had struggled so hard to live, but now she was with Grandma Gump and I knew she was happier than she was here.

On Sunday evening, my family all gathered at Mother's apartment and moved the furniture to its designated places. Dan and I arrived a few minutes early and there on Mother's dresser were her watch and glasses just as if she had taken them off minutes before. We cleaned out the apartment. It hit me as I drove away that my mother was really gone and there was no place left where I could visit her. It was such a wrenching, empty feeling.

Life continues even while dealing with a great loss. The first of August, Dan and I left for our annual two weeks in Colorado. Upon arriving home and driving into our Zanesville driveway on August 18, I noticed immediately that one of my magenta wave petunias along the driveway had a full gown pale lavender petunia growing in the middle of it. I had neglected my petunias all during June because I spent as much time as possible with Mom. The three weeks right after her death I watered and fertilized them and tried to get them healthy. Jasmine and Alicia had helped me weed them since I was in my power chair. But the pale lavender flowers were not there when we left for Colorado and I had watered each one carefully the night before we left. I remembered my conversation with Mother about what I wanted her to make bloom. I knew where the pale petunias came from. I went right out and took a picture of it. My kids soon learned about that flower and all came to look at it. Carrie knew she had never planted that color of petunia. We all marveled and saw my mother's hand in this.

But it did not stop there. In September, Zandra told me she had tried to grow wild flowers in the court yard of their pool apartment by sprinkling seed around but nothing came up. So it was a big surprise when just the week or so before, a white wild flower had suddenly bloomed. Burnie lived in the city and he took great pains with his yard. It is rather formal and pleasant. Now they had a corn stock growing in their yard. About that same time, I brought all my houseplants in because the nights were getting cold. Just days after I had brought in that long neglected orchid of Mom's, it grew a very long stem. And as I write this, the white orchid that has not bloomed since 1999 has six buds on it. I know there are logical reasons for these unusual happenings. But deep in my heart, I also know that Mother is in heaven and she is reminding me that love never dies.

Acknowledgements:

My sister, Zandra Bower is the reason this book was created and completed. She was the first to suggest the idea and never let me walk away from the project, even though I tried. Thank you to Dan, my husband and my daughters, Carrie and Rachel, who were my first proof readers. Along with Mike, my son and my brother Burnie, they all gave me valuable insights and the courage to continue. Much gratitude to Cynthia Hettinger for her patient and professional editing in helping me turn a family history into a story. Rhonda Gump's photography skills were greatly appreciated. Thank you Eileen Brodmerkel, your love of books and the English language have influenced many, including me.

To obtain an autographed copy contact:
Roxann Gump O'Brien
P.O. Box 8
Zanesville, IN 46799
email: roxob@aol.com